Shake Your Soul-Song!

A Woman's Guide to Self-Empowerment Through the Art Of Self-Pleasure

Devi Ward Erickson

DakiniDancerPress

Disclaimer ~

The information in this book is based upon the author's personal experience as an Authentic Tantra™ Educator, Certified Tantric Healer, and Sensual Dance Instructor. This book is for the purpose of educating and empowering women in their full sensual and sexual self-expression, and supporting each woman in connecting deeply to her own Inner Wisdom Guidance. The techniques and exercises described are to be used with the reader's discretion and reader's liability. The author is not responsible in any way for any experiences, issues, or injuries that may result from applying the methods contained in this book. Results from these methods are directly related to the amount of diligence applied.

Edited by: Alexandra Ward

Cover Design by: Katie Smith

Illustrations by: Kevin Furgerson

Quotes collected from: Pearls of Wisdom

DakiniDancerPress

ISBN-13: 978-0615708775

ISBN-10: 0615708773

Dedication

I dedicate this book to all women and men, for the purpose of their sexual healing, sensual awakening, and freedom from all forms of suffering.

Table of Contents

*There came a time when the risk to remain tight in the
bud was more painful than the risk it took to blossom."*

~ Anais Nin ~

Acknowledgements

I would like to acknowledge all of my Authentic Tantra® Sangha for their love, support, encouragement, and guidance.

I would also like to specifically thank Lama Tashi Dundrup of The Shangpa Kagyu Lineage for his instruction in the precious teachings of the Dharma, and for giving me permission to share some of those instructions.

I thank Jacques Drouin, my Tantric Consort and Co-Founder of Authentic Tantra® for introducing me to the path that leads to liberation, and being my most loving friend and supporter through my sexual healing and awakening.

I thank Jennifer Jones for her much appreciated and invaluable support and insight, in the various stages of this book. I thank Trina McGee and April Higgs for their friendship, encouragement and ongoing support. Roshini Bolar for awakening me to the power, beauty, and magic of Restorative Yoga, Babeland Toys for generously sending me some very wonderful sex toys to try during the formative stages of this book, and last, but not least, Mom, for not only using her wonderful analytical mind to help me edit this book, but also finding it interesting as she went along.

I would also like to thank all the other pioneers on the forefront of female sexual awakening that have shared their knowledge, insight, and experience though their work, much of which is listed in the back under Resources.

Forward by Lama Tashi Dundrup

I am definitely impressed with the quality of insight and compassion expressed in this book, written by a mature woman, who by connecting with her heart and her sexuality can bring other women to her level of accomplishment.

Most women have all of the right tools and abilities implanted in their bodies and inner states of consciousness. These instructions will bring them out in a way where they can value them and integrate them into their particular lifestyles.

Natural mind is defined by the experience of the female orgasm. There is nothing beyond this experience in the human mind.

Ah women!

Lama Tashi Dundrup, August 2012

Introduction

A Glimpse of The Divine

Our sexuality is a gateway to the divine. Literally.

According to the Vajrayana Tibetan Tantric teachings of the Shangpa Kagyu Lineage, the human body is designed such that every orgasm is literally a glimpse or "taste" of enlightenment.

They instruct that at the moment of orgasm, the moving pranas or "winds" in the genitals brush the central channel, (the core of the life-force in the body), and we get a *taste* of enlightenment.

Think for a moment of that brief, sweet, fleeting taste of bliss just as we orgasm –

> *Those few seconds of sweet freedom and pure ecstatic joy.*

What we are experiencing in *that moment* is a glimpse of our enlightened mind –

> *Our "true nature" as it were.*

But **what if** we were able to experience more than just a brief "glimpse" of orgasm?

What if we were able to extend and expand that moment of *pleasure* to last for several seconds, several minutes? ***What if*** we were able to touch that central channel over and over again, as easily as breathing, naturally and effortlessly?

What might that do for our bodies, our minds, and our

emotions?

It has been clinically shown that pleasure, be it physical, emotional, spiritual, but *especially* sexual, has a huge array of life-enriching physiological health benefits such as:

* Boosting infection fighting cells by 20% [1]

*Stimulating and increasing secretions of the pineal and pituitary glands, thereby positively affecting brain and body chemistry [2]

*Revitalizing the endocrine glands for more HGH, serotonin, DHEA, and testosterone production. DHEA is believed to improve brain function, balance the immune system, help maintain and repair tissue, promote healthy skin, and improve cardiovascular health. [3]

So *what if*, instead of feeling fear, guilt, ignorance and shame about our sexual and sensual pleasure, we understood it to be physically healthy, life-enriching, and supportive of our mental, emotional, and spiritual well-being?

What if we were able to experience pleasure as an internal

---

[1] Dr. Dudley Chapman, clinical professor of obstetrics and gynecology at Ohio University College of Osteopathic Medicine in Athens, Ohio, The Healing powers of Sex www.atus.net, 19 Aug 2001

[2] Candis Hale | Published 04/12/2007 http://www.ezilon.com/articles/articles/4699/1/The-Benefits-of-Orgasm%3A-Getting-Hot-and-Healthy!

[3] Chandi Devi http://healing.about.com/od/sexualhealing/a/tantricsex.htm

compass or guidance system, letting us know which actions were life serving, and which were not?

What if we gauged our life experiences not only by how much physical pleasure they provided, but also by how much emotional and spiritual pleasure we felt, so that having all "4 Forms of Pleasure" consistently met was considered vital to our entire well-being?

What if we could trust the voice of our heart and clearly hear the song of our soul?

What would life be like?

My Invitation ~

I invite you on a journey of self-discovery and soul remembrance.

I invite all women to dive deeply into the wisdom, vitality and passion of unrestricted sensual expression and soulful self-connection.

I invite you to reclaim the parts of yourself that have lain dormant and unseen, buried beneath the fear, pain and sensual ignorance of our cultural conditioning.

"Our deepest wishes are whispers of our authentic selves. We must learn to respect them. We must learn to listen."

~ Sarah Ban Breathnach ~

Part One ~

Sensual Awakening For Women

Chapter 1. Sensual Healing

We live in a culture that teaches women to both fear and ignore their sexuality and repress their sensuality. Authentic sexual expression is frowned upon in polite society, and though we can openly discuss the pro's and con's of yet another military invasion, we can't say the word "orgasm" at the dinner table, and the word "vagina" will get you thrown out of legislative discussions.

"Good girls don't and bad girls do", is a concept that is subversively present in our cultural orientation to female sexuality. This cultural admonition keeps us emotionally and psychologically reined in from fully expressing, or even exploring our sexual pleasure. We don't want to enjoy sex too much, "cuz only bad girls really enjoy sex."

And we as women absolutely do subconsciously ask ourselves "If I really enjoy sex, does that make me a bad girl?"

YES! According to our cultural programming, yes it does. And we all know what happens to bad girls. They get used, abused, raped, discarded, or simply shamed and treated with reproach and disdain.

There are serious repercussions in our culture for women who enjoy sex, much less fully own and embody their sexual expression. This is because our relationship to sexuality is wounded as a society, and, I believe, largely as a species.

Just Google "health benefits of sex" and you will see that physiologically, emotionally, and mentally, sex is one of the healthiest things we can do for our bodies, and our relationships. Yet it is often wrought with so much guilt, shame and emotional pain, that we avoid it entirely, or allow ourselves to enjoy it only minimally.

According to the Shangpa Kagyu lineage of Tibetan Tantric instruction, Human Beings are designed such that every orgasm is a glimpse of enlightenment. So quite literally, we are hardwired so that our sexuality *directly* relates to our spiritual realization.

How could there be shame in that?

I spent most of my adult life in a state of dormancy. I was emotionally and mentally crippled by deep, unrecognized, core wounding. This "wounding" or conditioning operated *below* my conscious mind, and therefore I was completely unaware of the fact that I was imprisoned by it.

This subconscious wounding or "trauma" held me tight in the grip of self-hatred, self-denial, lack of self-worth, and fear of self-expression. And yet, that was the state of being which I considered to be "normal". This is the state of existence which many people consider to be normal, experiencing just a mere fraction of their personal potential.

We are *internally bound* by subconscious restrictions on self-expression and culturally conditioned concepts of propriety. We see this most obviously in regards to sexual expression and sensual pleasure.

For me, freedom from this internal prison became possible when I began engaging my sexuality with conscious intention and *sacred awareness*. I became aware of these areas of subconscious core wounding, and these unrecognized, unrealized facets of my soul, which needed attention and healing in order for me to become fully integrated and "whole" as a human being.

It was through accessing my sexual and sensual potential that I have been able to access my personal potential, and I believe that this is true for every human being. I believe that only through consciously delving into the shadows surrounding our sexual fears, wounds, pains and pleasure will we become fully healthy, whole, and integrated as individuals, and eventually as a species.

What I offer to you in this book is medicine.

I share with you the tools that I myself have used and continue to use, to cultivate a deeply aware, intimately connected, and truly loving relationship to my sexuality, sensual pleasure, and the song of my soul.

If you deeply desire

- The freedom to explore and express your sensuality without fear, guilt or shame,

- To connect deeply with the song of your soul, and live a life that reflects the most pure, refined and authentic expression of your unique "soul purpose",

- To understand what your sexual energy is really about, and how to use that energy to access improved health, increased vitality, passion, pleasure and joy,

- To be free from the incessant internal chatter and emotional confusion that results from the battle of conflicting thought patterns between your conscious and subconscious minds,

- To easily access the internal inspiration and energy necessary to contribute meaningfully to the people in your life, and your community,

Then Shake Your Soul-Song is the path for you.

The key to the deepest, most profound connection with the voice of my own soul has arisen from and resulted from, everything I share with you in this book.

The key to accessing my personal human potential has been to consciously heal, engage, explore, and expand my sensual-sexual awareness.

It is an ongoing, life-long process of joy, self-discovery, and the experience of true freedom, which can only be obtained by coming to know, love, understand and accept yourself completely.

This depth of self-knowing and self-love is our birthright as women, sisters, daughters, mothers, and as human beings.

This depth of soul union is only achieved when we consciously integrate all aspects of our humanity, *especially our sexuality*, as sexuality is often the area of our deepest fear, deepest ignorance, and emotional, psychological and spiritual wounding.

"We do not see things as they are. We see them as we are."

~ The Talmud ~

My Invitation ~

I invite you on a journey of soul remembrance and reawakening, to the true power and purpose of your Nature-given, sacred, sensuality.

I invite you to reclaim the divine wisdom inherent within the female form.

I invite you to first uncover and then deeply connect with the voice and song of your soul.

Then I invite you to shake your soul-song fearlessly, in every area of your life.

"As we are liberated from our own fear, our presence automatically liberates others."

~ Marianne Williamson ~

Chapter 2. Soul Expression

My original intention for this book was quite different from what you are now reading. I suppose this happens for many writers, the original intention being in varying degrees different from the result. The original title was simply "The Art of Self-Pleasure for Women", and it was intended to be more of a mechanical manual for awakening the multi-orgasmic potential of every woman. It was a guidebook describing what our orgasmic potential is, why we don't experience it, how to cultivate it for ourselves, and how to reclaim our "sensual sovereignty."

Though that "mechanical" instruction is still included in this book (see chapter 19), "The 4 Principles of Self-Pleasure" are much more than a tool for awakening physical orgasm. They are a formula for activating our full human potential, creating inner balance, health, harmony, and achieving personal "soul" empowerment.

During the period of time that passed between the original concept of this book and the actual process of writing it, I myself inevitably underwent my own process of growth and transformation in relationship to my experience of pleasure. I began to experience pleasure not just in the context of my sexual life, but rather as an awareness to be cultivated in all areas of life.

I began to experience The Art of Self-Pleasure as a path to be followed, the awareness of it a skill to be cultivated, and the daily practice and awareness of it a discipline, or as my friend Trina Myra says, "a bliss-ipline".

"Follow Your Bliss", a term coined by Joseph Campbell, is much referred to in the world of modern, New-Age seekers. Though following my bliss is a great concept, the idea always left me with a feeling of unease and confusion, as being disconnected from my inner compass, I really had very little idea what my "Bliss" truly was, where to seek it, or how to find it.

It wasn't until I began to heal my relationship to my sensual expression that I began to unlock my bliss, and blossom into the full expression of my soul's purpose.

Sensuality is a *natural* expression of feminine essence. Because we are conditioned to fear and repress that inherent Life Energy within us, I believe we lose contact with some of the most precious and vital aspects of our Being.

Until we reclaim our relationship to our natural sensual expression, and have the inner strength and freedom to fearlessly express our sexual and sensual *pleasure,* we will remain disconnected, confused, and disempowered not just in our lives, but more importantly, within our own hearts and minds, separated from the true voice and song of our soul.

Reclaiming Our Sensual Potential

We are born into this world of sensory experience~ sight, sound, taste, touch, and smell. Each of our 5 senses also relates to the 5 elements ~fire, space, earth, water, and air ~ which make up our relative or "experiential" environment. As children we delight in our sensual experience. We want to taste it, touch it, feel it, understand it, *know* it. Those of us who have children, or have worked with small children, know that babies put almost *everything* in their mouths, as if to truly perceive an object, they need to not only see it, touch it, and smell it, they must taste it as well.

We learn about ourselves, and our environment *through* our senses, through our *sensual* experiences, and initially there is great joy in this process of self-discovery.

Our modern lives are filled with an overabundance of sensory stimulation, mental activity, and emotional overwhelm. In addition, many of us may have experienced painful childhood traumas such as physical, sexual, or emotional abuse. In order to cope with life, I believe we shut down a large degree of our sensual awareness, and disconnect from life itself. In our world of suffering and injustice, violence and conflict, I believe we numb-out to protect ourselves from the pain of being present in life.

The human design is such that we are built to survive, but there is a vast difference between surviving and *thriving*.

In his book The Mindbody Prescription Dr. John Sarno (a physician who specializes in pain relief) defined a disorder he named Tension Myositis Syndrome (TMS) to describe a variety of symptoms caused by external and internal stress, tension, and emotional repression. Interestingly during the course of his studies he found that *"awareness, insight, knowledge, and information were the magic medicines that would cure this disorder"*. [4]

It's commonly accepted that our physical state of health is directly related to our emotional and mental disposition towards life. "Pain Disorder" is considered to be a valid medical diagnosis for experiencing physical symptoms of pain, due to psychological and emotional stress, tension, anxiety, and trauma.

---

[4] By Kevin S. - 2006-04-13 http://www.disabled-world.com/artman/publish/sensory_overload.shtml

If psychological stress and emotional repression can cause physical pain *disorders,* what would be the effect of consciously cultivating pleasure and the awareness of pleasure in our lives?

The Art of Self-Pleasure is a 4-part formula for doing just that. It is based upon action-oriented, do-able *methods* for reclaiming the pleasure, sensual bliss and emotional joy inherent within us. This connection to life through sensual pleasure is our birthright and it is *hardwired* into the human design.

The Art of Self-Pleasure is about aligning ourselves with the ascending current of life within, and using that current to guide us to our personal passion, inner fulfillment, and soul satisfaction.

The Art of Self-Pleasure is a formula designed to support each and every woman in awakening to her true soul purpose and empower her to hear the whispered secret calling of her heart.

It is by recognizing the human vehicle as an "embodiment" of sensual awareness, and *pleasure,* that we can relax into our true nature, and trust the subtle impulse of life that arises within us.

We then reclaim what it means to be "woman": a vessel and portal for Life itself.

"Everyone has inside of her a piece of good news.

The good news is that you don't know how great you can be!

How much you can love!

What you can accomplish!

And what your potential is!"

~ Anne Frank ~

Chapter 3. Shaking Your Soul-Song!

Shake Your Soul-Song is written as a guidebook to support you in reawakening to the pleasure, joy, and sensual connection already residing within. I focus on giving practical, effective and enjoyable methods that you can engage in on a daily basis, to cultivate pleasure and the awareness of pleasure in your everyday life. Throughout this book I weave personal examples of how these methods have worked to heal my body, mind, and spirit, and radically transform my relationship to life.

I want to be very clear that I do not consider myself fully realized or "done" by any account. I consider self-realization to be a life-long *process,* and I teach that which I have had success with, and those methods that I continue to actively *do.*

My teacher Lama Tashi says "Teach what you know, teach from the experience of doing", and that is what I do. The knowledge that I have comes from experience, the experience of using the methods and teaching the methods over a period of several years. I also teach from the experiences that my students have shared with me, and how their lives have radically transformed, just by doing these simple little 'techniques' consistently over a period of time.

The proof of the pudding is in the eating, and I continue to be amazed at the healing, transformation and personal growth that people experience with The 4 Principles of Self-Pleasure.

The Format

I wrote this book in the same format that I teach my classes.

First, I give a clear picture of where we are at currently in our personal and cultural relationship to pleasure, sensuality, and female sexuality.

Next, I like to describe how we got to our current state, as I believe a situation cannot be transformed without understanding the root or *cause* of it.

Then lastly, I give you the medicine or formula for change.

Beyond *what* the medicine is, I also want you to clearly understand how and *why* it works. I believe that if we are able to understand how and why something acts to effectively create change in our lives, we are more likely to believe in and trust it, and subsequently we are all the more inclined to actually use it.

I recommend approaching this book as a journey of self-discovery.

I am a firm believer that change results from something that we actively *do*, and so I have included exercises in each of the chapters for integrating the teachings more deeply into your awareness.

I recommend starting a pleasure journal and using it in conjunction with this book. You will need it for completing the included exercises, and also to capture any "aha" moments that arise while you are reading the material.

I also recommend creating a support system of like-minded women to join you on your journey into sensual remembrance.

There truly is power in numbers, and in my opinion what the world needs most are groups of women everywhere who are questioning their conditioning, awakening from the bonds of sensual repression, and supporting each other in reclaiming their sensual sovereignty.

There are a number of ways that you can go about creating a support system:

A) One suggestion is to create a Shake Your Soul-Song reading group, where you read each of the chapters and do each of the exercises together as a group, (minus the partner and self-stimulation exercises, unless you want to!) In this way you are moving through the book material as a group, and can support each other through the entire process.

B) Another suggestion, which can be in addition to the one above, is to create a regular Shake Your Soul-Song 'practice group' to practice The Principles of Self-Pleasure together as a group (again minus the self-stimulation, unless of course that would meet your needs for shared pleasure).

Either of these suggestions would look like weekly, bi-weekly, or monthly gatherings where you would practice the Meditation and Movement together, and then have time for discussion to share about your deepening self-connection and awareness of pleasure in your life.

A possible format for the group gatherings could be:

2- 2.5 hours any day or night of the week-

1) Begin with meditation.

2) Check in by sharing what is meeting your needs for pleasure in your life right now, and also those things that are not meeting your needs for pleasure. I believe growth comes from acknowledging what isn't working, so that we can take action to make change.

3) Share any insights that you are having, i.e., any transformation, healing, etc. I encourage you to talk

about how your bodies are changing, how your awareness is opening, and *definitely* talk about your orgasms and what is occurring with your sexuality. In ancient times, when the art and practice of sexual Tantra was flourishing, women openly talked about their sexuality with each other as a way of learning and growing into sexual maturity.

4) Each person ends her segment of sharing with three appreciations about self and life.

5) Use the Feminine Emergence Dance DVD and practice The 5 Core Pelvic Movements.

6) Close with a pleasure that you would like to contribute to yourself and/or someone else the in the following days and weeks.

You can find more suggestions for furthering connection with other women on this particular path to soul empowerment, and receive ongoing support for you journey at my website www.Feminine-Emergence.com.

"There are two ways of spreading light. To be the candle, or the mirror that reflects it."

~ Edith Wharton ~

Chapter 4. Pleasure as a Path

All actions we take in life are determined by our motivation, our intention, i.e. what is the result that we are hoping and intending to achieve? For example, you are reading this book because you have a desire to learn, grow, heal, or become more self-aware in some area.

In 1943 psychologist Abraham Maslow developed a theory of human motivation termed "Maslow's Hierarchy of needs". He proposed that there is a hierarchy of core human needs or *values* that must be met in order for each human being to experience a relative level of inner peace and emotional balance.

Once these basic, core needs are met, there are other activities that can be focused upon in order to meet the greater need for "self-actualization". He calls these 4 foundational needs "deficiency needs" and states; "if these deficiency needs are not met the individual feels anxious and tense, and thus has very little motivation to focus on or address the higher or secondary need for self-actualization," i.e. "soul-purpose." [5]

Maslow defines "deficiency needs" as the core human needs such as:

- Physiological - food, water, sleep, sex, etc.
- Safety - security of body, of resources, of employment, of family, or health
- Love/Belonging - friendship, family, sexual intimacy
- Esteem - self-worth, confidence, achievement, respect.

---

[5]

http://en.wikipedia.org/wiki/Maslow's_hierarchy_of_nee ds

They are usually portrayed in the shape of a pyramid, with the largest and most fundamental levels of needs at the bottom, and the need for self-actualization at the top. *(See fig. 1)*

Fig.1

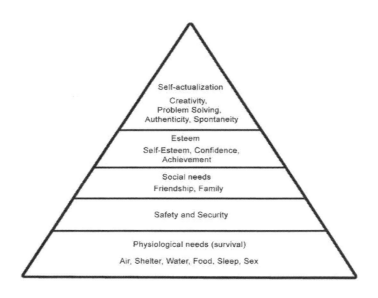

Maslow believed that all human beings have an innate desire

---

6 http://communicationtheory.org/wp-content/uploads/2011/01/maslow-hierarchy-of-needs-diagram.jpg

for self-actualization, and that this desire is literally "hardwired" into the human design. He coined the term "metamotivation" to describe the motivation of people who are actively seeking self–actualization, and striving to reach their full human potential.

He theorized that in order to meet our "meta" needs, our "deficiency" needs must also be being met with a large degree of consistency, otherwise we are too busy focusing on our basic needs for survival to have the residual energy necessary for pursing "higher" goals in life.

Some "Metaneeds" that we strive to meet in order to actualize our full human potential:

- Wholeness (unity)
- Perfection (balance and harmony)
- Completion (ending)
- Justice (fairness)
- Richness (complexity)
- Simplicity (essence)
- Liveliness (spontaneity)
- Beauty (rightness of form)
- Goodness (benevolence)
- Uniqueness (individuality)
- Playfulness (ease)
- Truth (reality)
- Autonomy (self-sufficiency)
- Meaningfulness (values)[7]

During the 1960's Dr. Marshall Rosenberg began developing a method of communication based upon Maslow's hierarchy of needs called Non-Violent or Compassionate Communication. Marshall theorizes that every human emotion or "feeling" is stimulated by one of these core human needs being met or unmet, by life circumstances or actions.

He suggests that if we are able to "follow the feeling" it will guide us to the need that is or is not being met, and from there we can develop clear strategies or actions to effectively address the core or "root" of the issue.

Without being deeply connected to our "feelings and needs" we wander around somewhat blindly, unclear about our motivations, and what life-enriching core values we are attempting to fulfill though our actions. (i.e. what is the outcome we are hoping to achieve?)

As a result of that inner lack of clarity, we often find ourselves

---

[7] http://en.wikipedia.org/wiki/Metamotivation

taking actions that do not effectively meet these needs, (or even directly address our core values), and this can lead to further frustration and dissatisfaction in life.

Without knowing and understanding our core motivations, we are unable to receive clear guidance from our internal wisdom voice, and are disconnected from our soul-song, our true soul purpose or calling in life.

Shake Your Soul Song describes living deeply connected to that inner voice of wisdom, and using that inner guidance to clearly recognize which needs are alive for us in each and every moment.

It encourages a life in which the needs for self-actualization and inner fulfillment are acknowledged as a primary and motivating force in life, and the only way in which true and lasting happiness will be achieved.

It means having access to the inner freedom and personal empowerment necessary to take actions that effectively meet those needs, and thus realize our full personal and human potential.

It means understanding that we are responsible for our own inner fulfillment in life. We can ask others to contribute to our happiness and joy, but they are not responsible for providing it.

Pleasure As Our Guide

I believe that the experience of pleasure is a built in "guidance system" designed to direct us on our own unique path of personal actualization and spiritual realization.

By following this thread of enjoyment, (a.k.a. *pleasure),* we will connect with and discover the magic that life has to offer us.

But the experience of pleasure is more than purely physical.

Many of our most fulfilling experiences of pleasure are also emotionally and spiritually pleasurable as well; like having a great meal with people that you enjoy, or contributing meaningfully to some else's life by donating your time and talent.

True Pleasure is an emotional experience of expansiveness that can spiritually align us with the "metastates of wholeness, union, beauty, goodness, etc."

Self-Awareness Exercise ~

1) Take a few moments to reflect upon your life, currently and in the past. Have there been times in your life when you "did things" or took actions in life without clearly understanding what your motivation was? What were the results?

2) Has there ever been a time in your life when you were very clear about your motivation, and took action to directly meet that "need"? What was the outcome? Did your action effectively meet that need, and if not, what might you have done differently to more accurately fulfill that desire?

"The best and most beautiful things in the world cannot be seen nor touched but are felt in the heart."

~ Helen Keller ~

Chapter 5. The 4 Forms of Pleasure

The human experience of pleasure has the potential to be a veritable symphony of seemingly infinite layers, colors, and textures. Each "flavor" of pleasure is unique unto itself, and yet rarely do we take the time to savor each of the distinctive forms and varieties of subtle sensation, which we are able to experience as human beings.

In this chapter I define what I call **The 4 Forms of Pleasure**. As you become more conscious of how and where The 4 Forms of Pleasure are appearing in you life, you may begin to notice that often two or more forms of pleasure are being experienced at the same time.

I believe this helps to distinguish pleasure from gratification, as rarely does gratification lead to emotional or spiritual *fulfillment,* whereas pleasure can be, and often is, a gateway to transcendence. (I discuss the difference between gratification and pleasure in detail in Chapter 8).

The 4 Forms of Pleasure are:

Physical/Sensual

Sexual

Emotional

Spiritual

1. The First Form Of Pleasure ~ Physical or "sensual"

pleasure - literally relates to the five senses of taste, touch, sight, smell, and sound. We tend to take this form of pleasure for granted the most, paying it an extravagance of attention in some areas, but not in others.

Think for a moment about how much importance you place on the sense of *taste* being pleasurable. Now how about smells? It's pretty crucial right? We instinctively avoid tasting and smelling things that are not enjoyable. This is part of the built-in guidance system of the human design, as bad tastes and smells can be an indication of something that would be harmful for us to ingest. Food which is spoiled, and could be potentially damaging for us to eat, both smells and tastes "bad" to us, i.e., not enjoyable. It would bring us no pleasure to eat rotten food, and could very well cause us great illness and pain, and even death.

Physical/sensual pleasure is the human body's way of communicating to our conscious mind about which activities are life-serving, and which activities could be potentially harmful, providing very simple and clear direction. Yet obviously there are exceptions, such as how fantastic Mc Donald's french fries taste and smell vs. how potentially dangerous they are to our bodies with their high fat content and lack of nutritional value. But I have experienced that the more I listen to and align with my subtle inner guidance system, the more clarity I have about what foods and actions will actually be healthy, positive and ultimately pleasurable for me vs. just satisfying (i.e., gratifying) a momentary or passing desire.

Conscious Sensual Awareness, (described in Chapters 6 and 7), invites us to place importance on cultivating pleasurable balance with *all* of the senses including sight, sound, and touch. We often neglect these other senses, or delegate them to "special circumstances" category, such as having the need for visual pleasure met only while we are on vacation in some gorgeous tropical resort, while living our day-to-day lives in dysfunctional clutter.

Though our life circumstances may not give us access to exceptional views on a daily basis, there are certainly some actions that we can take in our everyday lives to enhance our sensual experience in these other areas as well.

Some suggestions for enhancing other areas of sensual pleasure:

Sight

1) Make sure your home environment is tidy and find places to put clutter! Your external environment is literally a reflection of your inner state of mind, and it works both ways. By cultivating inner peace of mind, you will naturally want a more harmonious external environment, and cleaning up your living space can contribute to better mental clarity, focus, and inner peace.

2) If possible, adorn your environment with fresh flowers or flowering plants. Flowers are an ancient symbol for feminine beauty, and can be a visual reminder of those inner qualities of beauty, grace and abundance. If you are unable to have flowers or flowering plants, any type of live greenery will do

3) Invest in a piece of art that really connects you to the presence of beauty, grace, and feminine power, or better yet, make a painting or drawing that is an expression of your feminine creativity.

Sound

1) Create a sensual play list for yourself choosing only music that makes your heart swoon and soar.

2) Listen to the sounds of nature on a regular basis. No matter where you live, chances are there is some sort of natural music being played that you can connect with at least once a day, be it birds chirping outside your window, the sound of wind in the trees, or even the patter of rain outside your window. We tend to "block out" the tiny sounds of our natural environment, and yet we can use the subtle language of nature to become vividly present and aware of the inherent beauty of life.

3) Read your pleasure journal to yourself out loud. We call this "Tantric Speech." Expressing your pleasure in life-enriching language can literally be medicine for your ears!

Touch

1) The most obvious way to enhance this sense would be through some form of traditional massage, but I'm going to go beyond the norm here and suggest "Sensual Massage". Sensual Massage can be done with your partner, and the focus is not on deep tissue work, but more on the experience of receiving gentle, loving, and nurturing touch. If you are without a partner you can still benefit from healing touch by locating a massage practitioner in your area with whom you really resonate with. It is important to feel a sense of ease and trust with your practitioner because, if you don't to some degree emotionally trust the person giving you a massage, you will be unable to *fully receive*, and will experience only the most superficial benefits.

2) Hugs are a great way of meeting both physical and emotional needs for pleasure. Virginia Satir, who is often referred to as the mother of family therapy, declares that "We need four hugs a day for survival, eight hugs a day for maintenance, and twelve hugs a day for growth."

3) Never underestimate the sensual pleasure of warm water covering the entire surface of your body all at once. Long, hot, fragrant baths can be the source of much sensual enjoyment and positive pleasure chemistries in the body.

4) Feel the 5 Elements on your skin. Again, this is something we take for granted and rarely notice, except for in "special" circumstances like vacation or holiday. Next time you go outside, *feel* the wind or the rain. Embrace the sun on your skin. Lie on the ground and *feel* the earth beneath you. Our senses directly relate to each of the 5 elements in our environment. We can literally enrich the elemental energies in our bodies, (thereby enriching our overall health), by connecting more consciously with our environment.

2. The Second Form of Pleasure ~ Sexual pleasure - One of Maslow's four deficiency-needs is sex as a drive or function of the human body. But many people fulfill the physical need (gratification) without addressing their needs for *sensual* intimacy, the experience of which can be a gateway for expanded states of emotional and spiritual connection.

In my work, I encounter many women (myself having been one) who have barely glimpsed their true potential for sexual pleasure, and feel a deep sense of loss and emptiness regarding their sexuality. By actively cultivating a more sensual approach to our sexuality, we can bridge that gap between mere physical gratification and sexual *fulfillment*, creating a holistic, sacred sexual connection with ourselves, and our partners.

Some fun exercises for cultivating a more sensual-sexual experience can be found in the next chapter.

3. The Third Form of Pleasure ~ Emotional pleasure - The experience of emotional pleasure will often arise from having foundational needs such as connection, love, and acceptance met. Feelings of inner joy are an indication that the need for emotional pleasure is being met.

Some ways to meet your needs for emotional pleasure are:

- Giving hugs to people that you enjoy
- Verbally sharing your appreciation for people in your life (co-workers, friends, family, lovers)
- Taking time to notice and appreciate yourself
- Contributing to someone else's life in a positive meaningful way.

4. The Fourth Form of Pleasure ~ Spiritual pleasure - can also be referred to as *bliss*. We generally experience this form of pleasure when the heart is open and there is a free flow of energy between us and life. I call this the "Highest" form of pleasure, and have experienced that it can evolve from any of the other forms of pleasure, or simply arise on its own.

Becoming aware of how, where, and when each of **The 4 Forms of Pleasure** is making an appearance in our lives can support us in being vividly present and wholly engaged in life. By placing our focus on these small and simple appreciations, we begin cultivating our internal *ascending current*, which can carry us out of the "muck and mire" of our habitual thought patterns, and into more openness, presence, grace, beauty and love. A favorite saying of our Tibetan Buddhist Lama is "inside-outside-*same*," or in other words "thoughts are things."

According to most (if not all) New Age and ancient spiritual teachings, we literally create our reality with our conscious and subconscious thought patterns. "Change Your Focus and Change Your Life" is one of the many mantras repeated by New Age gurus again and again, for taking charge of your life and creating the reality that you want to be living. Though I agree with this concept to a degree, please remember that I am not advocating, "taking charge of your life" in an aggressive, driven, disconnected fashion.

I am extending the invitation to consider that- if what we focus on grows, (and I have found that yes, indeed it often does), what would happen if we increasingly put more and more of our precious awareness on all of the small, built-in ways that pleasure is an active part of our human existence? Maybe the pleasure in our lives would begin to grow bit by bit, and the pain and suffering would begin to loosen its grip upon our minds and bodies.

Imagine the world that could be created by women who were cultivating awareness of The 4 Forms of Pleasure in their everyday lives. It is part of our function as the divine feminine principle that whatever we cultivate internally, we naturally give to our partners, our children, our friends, and our communities. I believe that actively cultivating our pleasure-potential as women can be the key to healing ourselves, our families, our society, and humanity as a whole.

Using Pleasure to Activate our Potential

Interestingly, Maslow also described something called Metapathology, which is "the thwarting of self-development related to failure to satisfy the metaneeds. Metapathology prevents self-actualizers from expressing, using and fulfilling their potential. Reasons people may not become self-actualized include: poor childhoods, lower economic conditions, inadequate education, anxieties and fears."[8]

I propose that by invoking the essence of pleasure into our lives, we can transform some of these "Metapathological" tendencies within us. Pleasure can be used as medicine for healing, and experiencing any of The 4 Forms of Pleasure releases a complex set of hormonal responses in the brain that the body uses for supporting **physical, emotional, and mental health.**

Some of these life and health enriching, pleasure- generated chemicals are

- *Dopamine*
- *Serotonin*
- *Oxytocin*
- *Phenylethylamine*
- *Endorphins.*

Dopamine - is a neurotransmitter that generates *feelings of bliss*. Sexual Pleasure stimulates the release of dopamine in the body, but according to Naomi Wolf's new book <u>Vagina: A New Biography</u>, even just thinking about pleasurable sex and orgasm can cause this chemical to be released in a woman's body. "Few of us know that when a woman has an orgasm – and, even before that, when she feels empowered to think about pleasurable sex, anticipate it, focus on how to get it, and feels in control of and knowledgeable enough about her body to know she can probably reach orgasm during sex – her brain gets a boost of the neurotransmitter dopamine." She goes on to say- "This experience does not just yield pleasure, a fact

---

[8] http://en.wikipedia.org/wiki/Metamotivation

that is well known; it also *yields specific states of mind.*" [9]

Dopamine is also associated with reward, confidence, desire, motivation, sleep, mood, cognitive ability, attention, and focus.

Serotonin - is generally thought of as a "feel-good" hormone. It helps people feel relaxed, peaceful, happy and contented. Serotonin can be generated in the brain by pleasurable activities such as exercise (**movement/physical pleasure**), sunlight (**connecting with the elements/physical/sensual pleasure**), and **sexual orgasm**. Serotonin is also contained in wholesome foods containing high levels of vitamin B6 and tryptophan.

Oxytocin - is also known as "The Cuddle Hormone" because it causes people to form bonds and long-term attachments. Oxytocin is linked to personality, passion, social skills, emotional quotient, all of which affect career, marriage, emotional health, and social skills. Oxytocin is stimulated in the body through **touch and sexual orgasm.**

Phenylethylamine - is a neurotransmitter that has an anti-depressant affect, and helps us to feel more alert, and have a sense of well-being and contentment. It can be released in the body through experiencing **visual pleasure, sexual pleasure,** and is found in chocolate (!)[10]

Endorphins - are feel-good chemicals produced in the pituitary and hypothalamus glands in the brain. With over *20*

---

[9]Naomi Wolf, Guardian UK
09 September 12,
http://readersupportednews.org/opinion2/273-40/13380-a-new-sexual-revolution
[10]http://answers.yahoo.com/question/index?qid=20100219024916AAmKUXZ

different types of endorphins, they act as natural painkillers, lower stress, and improve immune system function. They induce a general sense of well-being, causing feelings of euphoria, and help us to relax! Some also increase confidence. Laughter, physical contact **(touch)**, exercise **(movement)**, and massage therapy have been shown to stimulate endorphin secretion. **Sex** is also a potent trigger for endorphin release. The practice of **meditation (spiritual pleasure)** can increase the amount of endorphins released in your body.[11] [12]

As you can see, nature designed us so that all **4 Forms of Pleasure** cause beneficial, life-supportive, mood enhancing responses in our bodies, brains, and emotional disposition.

In Chapter 9, I describe how the body will literally use the physical and emotional experience of *pleasure as medicine* to heal and release tension, stress, and trauma stored in the cellular tissue. This cellular release of trauma allows the pain held deep within our psyche to *let go*. This process of body-centered healing allows us to actualize more of our personal life potential by giving us the ability to access areas of subconscious wounding which we are unable to address on a conscious, intellectual level.

This approach to healing is called 'Somatic Healing' which is a specific modality that focuses on using breath, touch, movement, and awareness to integrate the mental, emotional, spiritual and physical aspects within each of us. Somatic Sex Education also incorporates the use of *sexual pleasure* as a

---

[11]

http://www.medicinenet.com/script/main/art.asp?articlekey=55001

[12]

http://science.howstuffworks.com/environmental/life/inside-the-mind/emotions/endorphins.htm vehicle for transformation, healing and emotional growth. I use some of the principles of Somatic Sexual Healing in Chapter 19 - "The Art of Self-Pleasure."

By actively using The 4 Principles of Pleasure since 2008, I have personally healed and released some of my early childhood sexual abuse trauma. This trauma was buried so deeply within, that I had no conscious awareness of it for most of my adult life, and yet it completely shaped the way in which I related to life, and shadowed my intimate relationships with men. Healing is an ongoing process, and though much of the physical abuse trauma has been relieved, there are still emotional repercussions that reverberate throughout my life, and perhaps always will. That being said, so much has already awakened and blossomed in my life as a result of the healing facilitated by these methods, and I feel excited about what other aspects of my Self will be uncovered and liberated as a result of my ongoing self-cultivation.

"Adversity has the effect of eliciting talents which, in prosperous circumstances, would have lain dormant."

~ Horace 65-68 B.C. ~

In Summary:

- *When we are meeting our own needs for pleasure we cannot go wrong.*

- *Pleasure (not gratification) is our built-in guidance system which lets us know when we are doing something life-serving, or life-defeating. We have been taught to fear our own internal compass, and thus divorce ourselves from our nature-given wisdom. The human blueprint is such that if it feels good to us, and it causes no harm to others, then the action or activity is most often life-serving.*

- *Experiencing all 4 Forms of Pleasure supports our physical, mental, and emotional health in concrete, measurable ways.*

- *The 4 Forms of Pleasure and their corresponding chemistries are:*

  1. Physical/Sensual Pleasure:
     a) Touch- Oxytocin, Serotonin, Endorphins
     b) Taste- Serotonin, Phenylethylamine
     c) Sight- Phenylethylamine

  2. Sexual Pleasure:
     Dopamine, Serotonin, Oxytocin, Phenylethylamine, Endorphins

  3. Emotional Pleasure:
     Dopamine, Oxytocin

4. Spiritual Pleasure:
   Serotonin, Endorphins.

My invitation ~

I invite you to engage The Art of Self-Pleasure as path of spiritual growth and personal healing, and allow it to lead you on your own unique journey of soul integration and self-actualization.

"Reality is what we take to be true. What we take to be true is what we believe.

What we believe is based upon our perceptions. What we perceive depends upon what we look for.

What we look for depends upon what we think. What we think depends upon what we perceive.

What we perceive determines what we believe. What we believe determines what we take to be true.

What we take to be true is our reality."

~ Gary Zukav ~

Chapter 6. Sensuality vs. Sexuality

This book presents the theory of using sensual pleasure as a pathway to personal realization and soul empowerment. For the purpose of maintaining clarity, I would like to define the word "sensuality" as I am using it throughout this book, and make an important distinction between **sensuality vs. sexuality.**

The word "Sensuality" has gotten a bad rap in our culture, and with no surprise, as when I looked up the official definition of the word "sensual" on dictionary.com this is what was provided:

1. Pertaining to, inclined to, or preoccupied with the gratification of the senses or appetites; carnal; fleshly.

2. Lacking in moral restraints; lewd or unchaste. *(!!!)*

3. Arousing or exciting the senses or appetites.

4. Worldly; materialistic; irreligious. *(Irreligious? Really?)*

5. Of or pertaining to the senses or physical sensation; sensory.

Given these definitions, it's no wonder that our cultural orientation to sensuality is so wrought with conflict, and the word itself is so frankly misunderstood.

As you can see from the definition above, the word "sensuality" is often mistakenly intertwined with "sexual gratification" and thus our cultural concept of "being sensual" is often interlaced with all of the fear, guilt, and shame we have associated with sex and sexual expression. But I would like to offer that sensuality is much more, and includes much

...tion to life, and in fact, the ...ess can radically *enhance* our ...as our sexual experience.

..., **Conscious Sensual Awareness** is one of the key elements missing in our modern lives, and one of the contributing factors to sexual dissatisfaction for both men and women.

"Conscious Sensual Awareness" means "Being aware of and fully present with the 5 senses of the human form: sight, sound, taste, touch and smell."

As I said in Chapter 1, the 5 senses are our receptors in life. They are our human body's way of interacting with the external environment, (sort of like our antennae, if you will), our way of perceiving and interpreting information about the world we live in.

As we mature from childhood, we become more accustomed to the magical nature of our senses, and begin taking them for granted. They begin to lose their initial mystical appeal, becoming "run of the mill" for us, and naturally so. It would be difficult, if not downright impossible, for us to navigate this planet with our senses as newly awakened as an infant's. If you have ever been on an acid or ecstasy trip, you can relate to how functionally debilitating it is to have our senses "stimulated" to such a heightened degree.

Yet, there is an aspect to *sensual balance,* which I believe is missing in our world, largely because of the cultural fear and disregard for most things "sensual". I believe this absurdly negative view of our sensual nature is due in part to fall-out from the Judeo-Christian, puritanical fore-founders of western culture. In order to keep their religious vows of chastity, (interpreted as spiritual purity) they abstained from most forms of sensory experience, with the sense-ual sensation of touch being the most obvious.

Depriving ourselves of the sensory experience of touch can be particularly detrimental; as recent studies have found that human physical contact is essential to the health and well-being of our human emotional, physical and mental development.

The act of touching and being touched releases endorphins, oxytocin and other "brain messengers" that act to:

- Reduce stress and fatigue
- Boost the immune system
- Ease pain
- Lessen depression and anxiety
- Slow the heart rate
- Lower blood pressure
- Increase circulation[13].

The miraculous healing power of touch has also been shown to help premature infants gain weight, and strengthen their immune systems. Studies have also found that human beings **deprived of touch** suffer developmental problems. Some experts have linked touch deprivation to compulsive behaviors, increased aggression and higher death rates.[14]

---

[13]Information complied from a variety pf sources including-
Mary Bauer, March 30, 2011 |
http://www.livestrong.com/article/186495-importance-of-human-touch/
Benedict Carey, February 22 2010
http://www.nytimes.com/2010/02/23/health/23mind.html
[14] http://www.livestrong.com/article/186495-importance-of-human-touch/

I believe that our fore-founders' religious recoiling from their natural sensory experience as humans created a deep wounding in the emotional and spiritual psyche of western (American) culture, and created an unhealthy, psychological division between sensuality, sexuality, and spirituality. I believe this internal divide runs contrary to the true nature and function of our human design, impedes our ability to realize our full human potential, and impairs our ability as a species to co-exist peacefully.

In truth, our sexuality is inescapably intertwined with our spiritual realization. The inseparable nature of sexuality and spirituality according to the Ancient teachings of Tibetan Buddhism is continuously referred to throughout this book.

Our senses ~ A gateway to presence

Freedom from the over-thinking of our intellectual minds can be found when we fully and consciously engage our sensory perceptions. Perhaps this is why our forbearers feared and reviled their senses so deeply. When we become present to our sensory experience, we become present in our bodies, and are momentarily *freed* from our habitual thought patterns, and our incessant internal chatter.

For example, take a few moments right now, and focus on your breath.

Feel, *sense*, the air coming in through your nose, and filling your lungs.

Feel your belly expand with each inhalation, and deflate with each exhalation.

Feel your ribs expand sideways as your body fills with the life essence that the air element brings.

Now where was your mind as you were becoming fully conscious of the sensual experience of breathing? Were you thinking of last night's dinner, tomorrow at work, or what so-and-so said on Facebook? Or were you too busy actually *feeling* the physical body that your consciousness inhabits?

Biofeedback studies confirm that energy goes where the mind focuses[15], and in those moments of attention to the sensory/sensual experience of breathing, all of our mental energy/focus goes there, to that one pristine moment, and we are entirely present with **no other thought**. This "present moment awareness" may last for just a split-second at first, before our habitual thought patterns take over again, but for that one, sweet moment, we are entirely present with our experience.

With practice of present moment awareness, our experience becomes such that, instead of connecting to life through a veil of thought, we are able to truly perceive and connect with the life essence available to us in each and every moment. Now that is a life well lived!

One of the main sufferings of our modern world is the over-functioning of our intellectual minds. Sensual awareness can be a vital tool for reconnecting to the present moment, through the "gateway of the senses" of the physical body.

In 1999 I began my spiritual journey in earnest, largely due to the enormous amount of emotional and mental anguish that I experienced from the *incessant* chatter of my mind. I found that connecting to my sensual *awareness* through dance, meditation, and especially through nature soothed my heart, and gave my mind a break from itself.

"Your vision will become clear only when you look into your heart...

Who looks outside, dreams.

Who looks inside, awakens."

~ Carl Jung ~

Self-Awareness Exercise #1 ~

In the same manner in which you became aware of your breath in the exercise above, take a few moments right now and focus on each of your five senses individually.

Starting with touch, feel your flesh press against the surface that you are sitting or laying on. Feel the fabric of your clothes touching the surface of your skin. Sense and feel the air in the room gently caressing your skin.

Moving to sound, listen to the sounds of life all around you: the sounds of the building or room that you are in, the hum of the appliances, the noise of your neighbors.

All of these are the sounds that make up our lives. Just listen and hear them without judgment of good or bad, right or wrong. Just observe and be present with your external reality.

Continue gently through all of your senses:

Sight- really look at your external surroundings. See the colors and shapes of the objects around you. Then look to see the space in which they appear.

Smell- Inhale the faint, subtle aromas of life

Taste- become present with the flavors and textures of liquids and food.

Enjoy the process of Awareness becoming aware of itself.

Now take a few moments to write about your experience. If you are practicing in a group, take a few moments and have everyone share what they experienced. Notice what came up for you. Did you find it difficult, easy, relaxing, agitating? Just notice how you felt. Whatever your experience was, it will change as you proceed through this book.

Self-Awareness Exercise #2 ~

I call this next exercise "Your Daily Bliss-ipline." I invite you to cultivate your sense-ual awareness by focusing on a different sense each day for 5 days. If you are focusing on the sense of smell, enhance your awareness of the *pleasure* invoked by that sense in your current everyday life situations. See how and where that sense pleasure is already alive and working in your life. Then observe how what you focus on grows, and discover how sense-ual awareness activates sense-ual pleasure.

"By cultivating our sense-uality, we quite literally enhance, enrich, and expand every aspect of our human experience."

~ Devi Ward ~

Chapter 7. Sex and Conscious Sensual Awareness

It is part of the human design to learn by example. Developmental psychologists confirm that children learn by imitating adults. Defined as "Social Learning Theory" by psychologist Albert Bandura[16], the behavior that we see modeled to us is often the behavior that we will reenact for the rest of our lives, whether it is beneficial or harmful.

"The cycle of abuse" is a testament to this particular process of learning, and sadly many of these learned behavior patterns are so deeply ingrained, that we are completely unconscious of the effect that they have on our disposition to, and experience of life.

What we see is often what we do, and in this culture there are very few resources for adults to view examples of healthy sexual intimacy, which clearly demonstrate our true sexual potential as human beings.

Most of the sexual intimacy that we see demonstrated is in the form of pornography, and though I do not have a negative view of pornography in and of itself, (I think if used with awareness it can be a healthy tool for sexual exploration, sexual intimacy, and arousal), I do not believe that it is a valid representation of authentic emotional intimacy, and mutually enriching sensual connection between partners.

In my work as an Authentic Tantra™ Coach and Educator,

---

[16] Albert Bandura, "The Bobo Doll Experiment" 1961 and 1963

one of the main complaints that I hear from couples is the lack of depth, intimacy and excitement in their sexual relationships. I believe this is in a large part due to the absolute *lack* of healthy sexual education available to us as sexually active adults.

The average time of sexual penetration, and this is considered NORMAL by the way, is 2-7 minutes. 2-7 minutes from the time the penis enters the vagina, to the time he ejaculates and guess what, ready or not, it's over!

I literally spend more time brushing and flossing my teeth every night.

Now, this 2-7 minutes does NOT include foreplay, which for most women consists of receiving some kissing, maybe a little breast rubbing, and some genital stroking for the sole purpose of "getting wet and ready" for those 2-7 fabulous minutes of penetration. Yippee!

The whole encounter takes maybe 10-20 minutes on average. We have very little visual reference, and therefore *mental reference* for sexual experiences that last beyond 2-10 minutes.

In her book Women's Anatomy of Arousal Sheri Winston describes how not having a visual reference for our sexual anatomy severely limits our sexual experience. In reference to female sexual anatomy and pleasure she states "Believe it or not, the majority of contemporary books and illustrations of female genital anatomy leave out most of the equipment responsible for arousal and orgasm. When these specialized sexual structures are omitted from the images and text, they're also absent from our mental model. **This limits your ability to access your full sexual potential—it's kind of like a**

psychological chastity belt."[17]

The same can be said for visual representations of our full sexual potential as human beings.

In movies we see hot, passionate sexual penetration lasting for maybe 30 seconds. He rips her undies off and penetrates her in the heat of passion (without any lube BTW, because women are supposed to be instantly wet!), makes a few furious thrusts against her pubic bone, and within *seconds* he orgasms, and they both collapse in intimate exhaustion, chests heaving with the exertion of intense passion.

Somehow this is supposed to be the deeply satisfying and enriching sexual intimacy we all strive to recreate for ourselves, even though it is more reminiscent of how my hamsters used to mate when in heat. 1, 2, 3 pumps to ejaculation, and boom! It's done. Lights out, show's over. Even those really intense and wonderful porn scenes last 10 minutes AT BEST.

Outside of a whole body "sensual massage", (which many people have never received), our sensual-sexual experience is very limited, and we really have no idea what we are missing.

So how do we create a more sensual-sexual experience for ourselves, and our partners, and experience more of our sexual pleasure-potential?

The answer is very simple. By practicing **Conscious Sensual Awareness.**

What happened when you focused on your breathing in the

---

[17] Sheri Winston, Women's Anatomy of Arousal: Secret Maps to Buried Pleasure, September 1, 2009.

exercises in the previous Chapter? Your surface-level mind slowed down, you became present in your body, and *aware* of the subtle sensations that are normally overlooked. You were present with and *felt* the sensual experience of your breathing process. If you were able to remain relaxed and focused, you may have become more aware of your other senses as well, such as sounds and smells. You may have moved your awareness to other areas of your body, and felt them tingle and "come alive" as you became more conscious to, and present with, this vehicle you call a body.

Now apply this to lovemaking. If both partners are cultivating 'sense-ual awareness', sex *slows down*. More focus is placed upon the pleasurable awakening of the senses, (think touch, taste, smell, sight, sound) than upon the end result of clitoral or ejaculatory orgasm.

I call this style of sexual expression "Sensual-Sexuality" and define it as

- *Exploring our sexuality with presence, innocence, curiosity and grace,*
- *Allowing the focus of our sexual experiences to be about cultivating pleasure, intimacy and self-discovery, and*
- *Rediscovering our sexuality as a playful journey into sensual wholeness and full soul expression.*

Conscious Sensual Awareness can enhance our sexual experience by giving the mind a tool for becoming fully present.

What is the number one key to becoming multi-orgasmic for both men and women?

It is present, relaxed awareness with focus, i.e., the ability to relax the body and focus the mind.

Focus the mind on what?

*Focus the mind on **pleasure** - the pleasure of the **sensual** experience.*

~ Conscious Sensual Awareness Partner Exercise ~

Below is an exercise that I developed for partners to cultivate sensual-sexuality. I invite you to approach the exercise with a sense of playfulness, curiosity, and discovery. This exercise is best done with both partners in their underwear or entirely nude.

I suggest giving yourselves 1 hour if possible so that you each have a turn, or if that isn't possible, scheduling 2 sessions of ½ hour each.

Begin with one person lying on the bed, either face down or face up, with the other partner sitting next to them on the bed. Please be sure that both participants are in a comfortable position, and that the temperature in the room is cozy.

Enriching Sight - Behold the physical body of the person who has chosen you as lover, partner and friend. View their form with loving eyes and appreciation for the gift of presence they bring to your life. Focus on the areas of their body that you find the most lovely to behold, be it hair, eyes, back, elbows, toes, whatever parts of their physical form you find particularly pleasing.

Enriching Sound - Now express your appreciation to them verbally. Praise and appreciation can be medicine to sooth the suffering caused by the "inner critic". We all have body image issues due to the unrealistic, culturally-enforced standards of beauty that we are exposed to everyday of our lives. Hearing loving words of acceptance and appreciation can literally heal our relationship with our bodies, on a deep emotional level. I give an example of my own physical/emotional healing experience with "Tantric Speech" at the end of this chapter

Enriching Touch - Breath energy into your hands and feel them come alive with intention. Now gently brush, rub, or stroke **down the front of your partner's body and/or up their back.**

(It is important to move in the direction that I suggest. By moving down the front and up the back, you are helping to balance the natural moving energies of the body).

Notice the contours of their flesh, the lovely lines, dips, and hollows. Send loving intention from your heart, through your hands, as you honor the physical container for the heart and soul that you adore.

Enriching Smell - Again following the direction of moving up the back and down the front, smell your lover from head to toe, taking the time to smell all the pulse points, and detect the subtle differences to be found in each area of the body. For many people the natural scent of their lover can be highly arousing and the experience of being consumed through smell can be seriously erotic!

Enriching Taste - Following the directional patterns of movement, (down the front and up the back), kiss and taste every inch of their flesh. Starting from the tips of toes, to top of the head and back down again. Pay special attention to the areas that you were particularly drawn to by smell. Humans are wired such that if something is edible, and we like the smell, chances are we will enjoy the taste as well.

(You can also use this exercise to inflame sensual passion outside of the bedroom, by really *tasting* your partner's mouth when you kiss. The same can be done with the other sense exercises as well.)

When you are done, take a few moments to share with each other about your experience. Be sure to share emotions that arose as both the giver and receiver. Share any feelings of love, appreciation, and discomfort, whatever arose for each of you. We cultivate deep soul intimacy with each other when we are able to put words to the inner workings of our hearts, and share them with someone we love.

*Note- For further cultivation of sensual sexuality, I recommend the sensual-sex education offered through Authentic Tantra.com. My partners at Authentic Tantra and I devoted over half a year to compiling and filming the most authentic, sensual, healing, and powerful Tantric sexual education available, to provide one of the most comprehensive learning experiences available online, anywhere in the world. You and your partner can have instant access to this instruction 24 hours a day, 7 days a week, for an entire year from the date of purchase. This gives you plenty of time to view and review the material, in the comfort and privacy of your own home, and at your own pace.

"Love looks not with the eyes but with the mind and therefore is winged Cupid painted blind."

~ William Shakespeare ~

The Healing Power of Sound ~Appreciation and Tantric Speech

My own experience ~ I am a bi-racial woman, with Mom being Polish and Slovakian and Dad being African American, Native American, Irish, English, and god knows what else. Apparently I am "built like a black woman", meaning muscular, stout, and not thin and "waif like". I am naturally curvy, and have been so since about 14 years old.

Growing up in predominately white neighborhoods, my culturally conditioned orientation to female attractiveness was based upon that value system (WASP), which meant basically –the skinnier the better, and small round butts were best.

I have what is fondly referred to as "a ghetto booty" and though I was, and still am in fairly good physical shape, I did not fit into the *desired* category of body shape or type.

Needless to say, I had some fairly negative internal dialogue going on about my body and my booty. Indeed I spent most of my life struggling with really painful body-image issues and self-criticism.

When I initially began practicing Authentic Tantra with Jacques Drouin, my body image issues were so debilitating that I could not bear having my rear end touched in any way whatsoever. I also consciously managed how I walked, so that my butt wouldn't jiggle "too much", for as we women know, there is nothing more unsightly than a jiggly ass.

Jacques Drouin on the other hand LOVED my butt.

He fantasized about my butt, adored it, worshipped it, and because he was not permitted to touch it, due to the physical pain and emotional discomfort I felt from being fondled in that area, he was forced to express his appreciation through words. And so he did. Every time I saw him, which was several days a week, for hours at a time, he verbally expressed his love, appreciation, and downright adoration of my large, round, and beautiful bum.

At first I felt *really* uncomfortable upon hearing these expressions of joy and appreciation, then less and less so, until gradually I began to enjoy hearing what he had to say about this area of my body.

Over a period of time, I noticed that my movements as a dancer changed, my pelvic movements were more open, and I began including butt jiggling dance moves in my Sacred Erotic Dance class choreography (which was previously unheard of!)

I also noticed that I didn't mind, (and eventually even enjoyed!) having my rear end rubbed, stroked and massaged, whereas before I had experienced it as both emotionally and physically painful.

It was then that I discovered the true power of positive speech, and how words can literally heal our relationship to our bodies.

"What comes from the heart, touches the heart"

~ Author Unknown ~

Self-Awareness Exercise ~

1. Take a few moments and look at yourself in the mirror. This can be a difficult exercise I know, as that critical voice inside tends to kick up a notch when we see our physical image. (If you can't do this exercise while looking at yourself in the mirror, then just do it in your journal.)

2. Next, observe three things that you appreciate about your physical body. It can be anything, hair, eyes, nose, lips, teeth, the skin on your shoulders, your earlobes, whatever. If you can't find three things, then start with one.

3. Now speak this appreciation out loud to yourself, while looking at yourself in the mirror.

4. Say to yourself "I appreciate my. ......_, and am grateful to have them/it".

5. Repeat each appreciation three times before moving to the next. If you find more than three physical attributes, then by all means, list them all. In my opinion, the more positive things we say to ourselves about ourselves, the better!

6. Now in your pleasure journal, share how you felt during the experience, and how you feel after. Whatever your current experience is, allow for it to change as you proceed through this book.

"Whatever a person's mind dwells on intensely and with firm resolve, that is exactly what he becomes." ~ Shankaracharya

Chapter 8. Gratification vs. Pleasure

Much of the social and religious conditioning that we receive in this culture encourages us to perceive pleasure as something dirty, wrong, or shameful, especially when it involves *sexual* pleasure.

I find the term "Guilty Pleasure" quite telling in that it reveals the inner conflict so many of us experience when meeting our core human needs for pleasure. But it may be that when we are engaging in what we call "a guilty pleasure" we are subtly aware that the activity does not really meet our need for pleasure, but simply *gratification* of desire instead. Even though there is nothing inherently wrong with gratification, I do consider there to be a distinction between "gratification" vs. "pleasure".

Gratification vs. Pleasure

Gratification is similar to feeding a physical craving, or even an addiction. It is generally self-oriented in motivation (egoic self), and is based upon using an outside, external experience to satiate the hunger *inside*. I define it as more of a carnal/physical impulse.

Energetically I compare gratification to a low-grade clitoral orgasm: short, fleeting, superficially satisfying, and with no real lasting resolution or depth.

Pleasure, on the other hand, is more than a mere fleeting physical sensation or momentary satisfaction. **It is an emotional experience that can be a gateway to expanded states of self-awareness, bliss, joy, and spiritual realization.**

Pleasure can often be stimulated from external experiences,

but it has an energetic *quality*, which can be breathed in, savored, and absorbed into the very essence of our Being-ness, so that we in turn radiate it back out into our environment. It is an experience that often times is enhanced through sharing, and generally results in a more open-hearted experience of life.

During the course of writing this book I made sure to fill my pleasure reservoirs to overflowing. I began my days hiking in the beautiful red rock deserts of Sedona, Arizona. I climbed various mountain outcroppings to meditate on spectacular views that deeply nourished my soul on every level. I allowed the visual pleasure of the environment to fill me up, breathing in the essence of each of the 5 elemental energies, allowing them to activate, enrich, balance, and heal my body, mind, heart and soul. I then carried this inner fulfillment into my life, and used the joy, inner peace and pleasure to write this book, perform coaching sessions, and schedule interviews. By meeting my need for sensual connection with the environment, and reveling in the experience of sensual pleasure, I was filled with an inner sense of ease, peace and personal joy that I was then able to transfer to other areas of my life.

When we are aware of how, when and where The 4 Forms of Pleasure show up in our lives, we can use that awareness to access more creative passion, power and fuel for life. Accessing sensual pleasure does not have to happen only in the context of extravagant experiences such as time-share resorts in Sedona or luxury vacations in Hawaii. Sensual pleasure can be accessed most effectively and poignantly through the simple experiences of our everyday lives.

As I described in Chapter 6, simply becoming vividly aware of each of our 5 senses can be a gateway to present moment awareness, and the magical gift of being in physical human form. Also, finding simple things to praise and appreciate about our physical experience begins to generate a new relationship with life, in which we come from the standpoint of the glass being "half-full" rather than "half-empty".

"We shall not cease from exploring, and the end of our exploring

will be to arrive where we started and know the place for the first time."

~ T.S. Eliot ~

Chapter 9. Pleasure As Medicine

In Authentic Tantra™ we have a saying that Pleasure IS Medicine, and generally we are referring to using the sensation of sexual pleasure to heal and release emotional trauma stored in the genital tissue, which may be impeding our ability to fully experience sensation, as well as limiting our orgasmic potential. This concept of using "pleasure as medicine" can also be applied to every other area of our lives.

But what makes pleasure medicinal? How and why does it work to effectively heal and transform our mental, emotional, and physical bodies? The answer can be found in the way the body and mind work together as one system.

Think for a moment about a really painful life experience that you have had that still carries a charge for you. Since we tend to forget physical pain more easily than emotional pain, for this exercise, focus on an emotional pain, such as a heartbreak, loss, or perceived injustice. Now meditate upon that experience for a few minutes. Really get in there, and conjure up the visual memory, as if the entire experience were occurring again, right now, in this very moment.

Notice how your body feels. Notice the tension, the shortness of breath, the clenched jaw and possibly even gritted teeth. Notice how tight and *contracted* everything has become, your mind, your body, your awareness. Notice your heart beating faster, and possibly even your adrenaline pumping, just from remembering this event in your past. You may have experienced a hot surge of anger flaring up inside, or tears well up as you conjured this memory of an event, *that no longer even exists*, except as this emotional and chemical response occurring in your body.

Now change gears and think of a pleasurable experience. I happen to love hot scented bubble baths with candles, so one of my favorite images to conjure up is that of a nice, big, marble tub, with candles lit all around, fragrant with essential oils, and soft classical music playing in the background. It's been a long, full, satisfying day, and I am home alone, with nothing to do for the rest of the evening but enjoy my bath.

If this imagery appeals to you, then I invite you to focus on imagining those first few moments of slipping into this sweet, warm, sensuous experience. The sounds of pleasure, relaxation, and release that you would make as your whole being opens in bliss, and you settle into the soothing embrace of this experience. Feel how your heart expands, the tension releases, the body opens, and the subtle, internal contraction melts away. Feel how the cells themselves open and yield to offer up the pain they have been holding onto, and allow it all to melt and fade away to relaxed bliss.

Now take a few moments to notice the contrast between how you feel in this moment of conjuring pleasure, to the moments before of recalling a painful experience.

All of our life experiences, whether painful or pleasurable, can leave emotional imprints within us, as you just observed. These emotional imprints are stored in the cellular tissue of our bodies, and painful life experiences will reside there, as unresolved tension or "trauma". Just by *thinking* of the examples above, your body was reacting to the memory/imagery as if the experience were *actually occurring*. The imprint of the experience stored in your cellular tissue is what we call *cellular memory*. It is beyond the conscious mind, and is part of the inherent intelligence of the human design.

Painful life experiences that get trapped in our cells cause that tissue to recoil, contract, harden, and become what Margo Anand[18] refers to as "body armor". Body armor is just that. Acting like a shield to protect us from further pain, it shuts down our ability to feel and receive sensations, both physically and emotionally. And yet it does so at a dear cost. The body and mind are not separate, they in fact function as a whole most effectively, and so if we are armored in our hearts and minds, our bodies are armored and shielded as well.

In her paper Somatic-Experiential Sex Therapy: A Body-Centered Gestalt Approach to Sexual Concerns, Stella Resnick, PHD, discusses the process of body armoring from a somatic healing standpoint. She says, "Whenever there are sexual issues of an inhibitory nature, the fear, shame, guilt, trauma, and negative thought patterns are all locked in the body in a *defensive reaction* to the possibility of sexual contact or interest. This is true regardless of the past events that instilled these feelings, or the current inner narratives that sustain them. Ultimately, it is the physical constriction that blocks contact. That means whenever such an individual encounters a potential sexual situation or begins to feel turned-on, he or she is likely to hold the *breath and tense the body*.[19]"

According to the principles of Somatic Healing this internal contraction occurs from *any* kind of emotionally traumatic or painful event, be it sexually related or otherwise.[20] So how can we use pleasure as medicine to correct this "defensive

---

[18] Margo Anand "The Art of Sexual Ecstasy", page 128, Penguin Putnam1989
[19] Stella Resnick, PHD, Somatic-Experiential Sex Therapy-A Body Centered Gestalt Approach to Sexual Concerns. Gestalt Review, 8 (1): 40-64, 2004
[20] Emotional Anatomy, Stanley Keleman, 1985 Center Press, Berkeley

reaction" pattern?

As I pointed out in Chapter 5, when we experience any of The 4 Forms of Pleasure, we get a blissful "rush" of **Dopamine, Endorphins, Serotonin** and other neurotransmitters that stimulate feelings of joy, *relaxation*, contentment, happiness, confidence, etc. In addition, these naturally-produced chemicals effectively act as pain relievers, anti-depressants, and stress relievers.

The experience of pleasure allows our emotional and physical bodies to heal by supporting the entire mechanism of mind/body/spirit in letting go of the unconscious internal tension, which results in body armoring. Our *natural response* to the experience of pleasure is to relax, release, yield and open. When we allow ourselves to *fully feel* our own pleasure, we give the body a chance to heal itself by allowing the cellular tissue to purge the residue of mental, emotional and physical pain that has been trapped there for so long, and often without us even being aware of it.

By relaxing, releasing, yielding and opening through pleasure we become a conduit for Life to flow through.

"The Snow Goose need not bathe to make itself white.

Neither need you do anything but be yourself."

~ Lao Tse ~

Chapter 10. Finding Your 10 spot!

Your "**10 spot**" is a term I like to use to help us more clearly identify what is or is not meeting our needs for pleasure, in any given moment, and also, how effectively those needs are actually being met.

The concept of a "10 spot" can be found in many a self-help book or magazine article, but the idea was originally introduced to me by one of my Tantra instructors, Carla Tara. In Tantric practice, we generally use the 10 spot as a way of facilitating clear communication between partners about our sensual-sexual pleasure.

I began applying this concept to other areas of life outside of sexuality, when a student of mine was talking about her workday, and using the scale of 1-10 to share more intimately with her partner about the level of enjoyment she had experienced throughout the day. I thought that was a radically fabulous idea, and so I borrowed the concept and expanded upon it to present the model that I currently use, and now share in this book.

So what is your 10 spot? Think of your pleasure on a scale from 1-10, with 10 being the most pleasurable, 1 being the least. Now, think of where you are right this very moment on a scale from 1-10. Are you completely comfortable reading this book right now, with your head and neck supported, your feet up, and pillows beneath your lower back for support? Or do you have tension in your neck and shoulders; is your foot asleep, your leg cramped, etc?

The concept behind the "10 Spot" is simply to "check-in" with ourselves at any given moment, and find out where we are at mentally, emotionally, and physically on a scale of 1-10. If we are not experiencing the *most* comfort, bliss and pleasure that we are capable of feeling at that moment, then ask ourselves, "what would make this experience a 10 right now?"

Now granted, there are times when a 10 is just not possible. The causes and conditions of the experience simply will not warrant a 10, no matter what. I am reminded of an experience recently where I was attending a Canada Day Parade.

I was there with a friend, and we were enjoying the passing stream of colored floats, skipping children, and costumed people dancing by. My friend asked me where I was at on a scale from 1-10. I checked in with myself and responded with "a 7". She asked me what would make this experience a 10 for me, and after a few moments of reflection I realized, nothing. The circumstance simply was not going to be a 10 for me no matter what occurred. I was warm enough, my tummy was contentedly full, I was with people that I enjoyed, but the overall experience was simply not a 10 on my scale. And that was perfectly okay. I was content to be present for the remainder of the experience, knowing that a 7 was all that it had to offer.

Conversely though, the previous day I had a very poignant experience of the subtle emotional and psychological undercurrents sometimes involved in granting ourselves a perfect 10. I was on vacation with said friend, on the Sunshine Coast of British Columbia, Canada. I had been working for weeks, (months actually) without a break, and on the first day of vacation my body took the opportunity to catch up on some much needed rest.

I spent the entire day meeting my need for pleasure by reading some cloak and dagger detective/thriller novel. I sat upright in a chair like a proper adult *should* while reading a book during the middle of the day, but eventually I made my way over to the bed to lay down on my side, which is my favorite way to just zone out.

As I was laying on my side reading, (thoroughly enjoying my book), I realized that I was just a wee bit chilly, and would probably be more comfortable under the covers. I recoiled at this idea, somewhat ashamed of myself for thinking of climbing under the covers during the middle of the day. What would people think? How would that be perceived? I surely didn't deserve to be THAT comfortable! I attempted to convince myself to just be content with the degree of comfort and pleasure that I was currently experiencing, and not push my luck by asking for more. All of this inner dialogue I registered on a subtle, almost imperceptible level. After several minutes of being aware of *almost* perfect comfort, but not quite, I finally consciously asked myself "what would make this a 10 right now?" The internal answer came back "a blanket". With that clear, definitive answer, I let go of all of my self-judgment and recrimination, got myself a blanket, and snuggled down to blissfully and thoroughly enjoy my "10 spot."

At the moment I achieved my 10 spot, I felt a deep release of internal stress that I had been unconsciously holding onto, and my body let go into a state of deep relaxation that is similar to what I have experienced during Restorative Yoga sessions.

A word about Restorative Yoga - An integral part of my self-pleasuring recipe, Restorative Yoga literally uses physical support as pleasurable medicine, for deep healing and release of internal tension. By giving the body the support it needs, it allows the nervous system to reach profound states of relaxation, which are not possible to experience by any other means. It was introduced to me by Roshini Bolar, and has been profoundly healing for my emotional body, and deeply transformative for my approach to life in general. It has been through my work with Roshinsi Bolar and Restorative Yoga that I have more fully awakened to my 10 spot in every situation in life.

The answer to what and where our "10 spot" is in every moment comes from deep inside our own hearts. Our inherent wisdom awareness will guide us to meeting our own needs for pleasure, if we pay attention to our subtle natural desires, and allow them to be fully expressed.

One of the ways in which I determine whether a desire is an authentic expression of my soul or not, is by asking myself "will fulfilling this desire cause harm to myself or anyone else?" From there I can usually determine with clarity if fulfilling that internal impulse is truly "right action" and if it will be in my best interest to act upon.

When coming from our inner alignment, our "10 spot" has the potential to guide us to our deepest sources of nourishment. It is important to be aware of the critical voices inside that may prevent us from hearing the clarity of our internal guidance. I suggest that if you are uncertain about whether an action is in alignment with your soul, to simply ask yourself "will this action cause harm to myself or others?" From there you will have the wisdom to choose what 'right action' is for you.

As I described above there are various reasons we have to *not* grant ourselves permission to receive our 10 spot in life, and I outline them in more detail below:

1) **I don't deserve it** - Generally we are not *consciously aware* of our thought patterns regarding meeting our

needs for personal pleasure. "I don't deserve pleasure" is certainly not a mantra that we *consciously* invoke on a daily basis. Yet much of our resistance to finding, exploring, and communicating about our 10 spot in life comes from the subconscious belief that we don't truly deserve the happiness and pleasure that we all so desperately crave. Here's a great way to find out if your resistance stems from feelings of unworthiness. On a scale from 1-10, how guilty do you feel when thinking about scheduling in 30-60 minutes of "me time" a day? This question brings us to our next reason for holding out on our 10 spot in life....

2) **There's not enough time** - Yes life is busy. Busy, busy, busy. Always something to manage, oversee, fix, change, etc. I know. I am a self-employed workaholic. I will work 14 hours a day with no break until I collapse into a shivering mess on the floor, *if* I am not *consciously* cultivating balance in my life, by meeting needs for self-care and self-pleasure. Happily (and somewhat surprisingly at first), I found that when I do create time and space in my life to meet needs for pleasure and enjoyment, in healthy conscious ways, it enhances my ability to contribute more effectively in life, and increases my productivity at the work I love so much.

Example ~ As I am writing this book, I am balancing my need for self-pleasure with my need for self-care and productivity, by taking breaks to swim in the pool, exercise in the fitness room, and read a thriller novel, just for fun. Granted, this is a rather elaborate set-up I have here, so when I am in my "natural' environment, I make sure to meet my needs for self-care by practicing The 4 Principles of Self-Pleasure on a consistent basis.

It is just as important for us to schedule in our "me time" as it is for us to schedule in every other aspect of our lives. I myself would often not consider my "self-time" to be as important as "work time" or "partner time", and so it would more often than not get overlooked or compromised, as I prioritized contributing to others' lives above my own. It wasn't until I began to MAKE time by scheduling it in, (and sticking to it!), that I really began to experience the positive, regenerative effects of pleasure in my life, and began to have a clear understanding of how cultivating my own pleasure-potential enriches every other area of my life. Consistently observing my "10 spot" in all areas of my life has created an inner sense of fulfillment and soul connection that blossoms from the inside out.

3) **It's not okay, i.e. I don't have permission** - As I described in my previous example, I initially denied myself the super cozy 10 spot of being under the covers while reading my book, because I didn't think it was "appropriate" to want that. I didn't need to be *that* comfortable, and to ask for more was just "pushing my luck". I was coming from the internal program that told me "If I had any worth whatsoever I would have been up and out and doing something," *not* listening to what my body really wanted, and giving it the rest it deeply needed. By giving myself permission to experience my FULL pleasure-potential in that moment, I was able access a deeper level of healing and *nourishment* for my body, heart, mind and soul.

4) **Just get though it or "fuck through it"**- Just get through it, or as I often say in my works shops "just fuck through it", is a common attitude that many

women unconsciously subscribe to, especially in regards to sexual pleasure. If you take a moment to think about how many times you have been having sex and been slightly uncomfortable physically, be it due to dryness, awkward angle, a little pain during penetration, etc. Or maybe emotionally, you were feeling slightly (or severely) disconnected, numb, shut down, and just tried to push the feeling aside and ignore it. I call this "just fucking through it" when we silently endure a situation, hoping the discomfort will go away, or thinking to ourselves "it will be over soon, so why bother". Often we override or just plain ignore what's really going on for us in the moment, in order to "please" our partner. We don't want to disturb the mood or "rock the boat" by acknowledging and communicating about our pleasure, or lack thereof. I believe this ties into how we are culturally conditioned as women to

> a) Be largely disconnected from our sexual/sensual pleasure, (we aren't *supposed* to know what we like) and

> b) Feel shy or fearful about asking for sexual pleasure due to an inherent lack of sensual self-worth, i.e., "my sexual pleasure is not important", and/or an attitude of "I'll take what I can get"

Also, please do keep in mind that the average time of sexual penetration (penis in vagina) is a mere 2-7 minutes, and thus many of us have simply never had the time to discover what and where our sexual 10 spots are. We simply have no frame of reference for any kind of sexual pleasure experience, other than the one we are accustomed to having on a regular basis. In short, we don't know what we don't know.

I myself was a classic "fuck through it" type. Pain during penetration was expected. Not excruciating pain, but a subtle sharp pain during the initial penetration, and tender spots throughout were pretty much par for the course. I thought my "role" as a good lover was to lie on my back and moan really loudly to let my partner know he was doing a good job.

I was somewhat numb for the initial 2-7 minutes of sexual intercourse, and then, just when I started to really FEEL the sexual energy move, the man would ejaculate, and the experience would be over, leaving me feeling frustrated, aroused, and wanting more. I often couldn't wait for him to go home so I could masturbate, giving myself a clitoral orgasm to relieve the pressure of unsatisfied sexual hunger. Instead of craving my own orgasm during penetration (which I did not even believe was possible), I craved his semen, using the creamy feeling of connection I got from his ejaculatory orgasm as a substitute for sexual satisfaction.

I believe the remedy for our lack of personal and sexual satisfaction as women lies in understanding our cultural programming regarding our own pleasure, and being willing to reclaim our Sensual Sovereignty and create a New Pleasure Paradigm as I describe in Chapter 12.

Self-Awareness Exercise ~

1. Take a few moments to observe where you are on a scale from 1-10 right now - physically, mentally, emotionally, on every level. Now, ask yourself "what would make my experience a 10 *right now*?" Then, if you are able to meet that need for yourself, do it. Achieving your 10 spot in this moment could be as simple as putting a pillow behind your head, covering up with a blanket, or getting a glass of water.

    Some experiences simply do not have the potential to be a 10, no matter what you do. If that is the case, then just be present with what is, as it is.

2. Next, make a commitment to yourself to observe your 10 spot in different areas of your life. Some instances are:
    *   While eating any meal
    *   While watching TV
    *   While driving
    *   While having sex or self-pleasure
    *   While exercising.

    Take a moment to check in with yourself while engaging in any of these activities and determine if there is a higher level of pleasure that you could be experiencing. Again, experiencing your 10 spot could be as simple as adding some salt to your food, having a sip of water, or adding a little more lube.

Remember ~

You are worth a 10.

We all are.

"Women need real moments of solitude and self-reflection to balance out how much of ourselves we give away."

~ Barbara De Angelis ~

Chapter 11. The Walt Disney Syndrome

If you have ever watched a scary movie you know that usually the first person to get killed by the psycho axe murderer is the girl who has sex. She's usually the bubbly, giggly, provocative one in really short shorts, who has no qualms about "going all the way", while the girl who survives the slaughter is the one who has retained her chastity, and denied the sexual advances of her male suitors.

This may seem insignificant all on its own, but this is a common theme that runs throughout all of the cultural media that we are exposed to, from the time that we begin listening to bedtime stories and Walt Disney fairytales, to the time that we read teen novels, and Harlequin Romance. We receive our education or "guidance" in this culture about what is socially acceptable behavior for men and women to engage in, through our stories, our television shows, our movies, and other forms of media. We are repeatedly shown images that first suggest to us preferred behavior patterns, and then reinforce that suggestion again, and again, until it becomes a subconscious belief system that we are operating from, without even knowing it.

Advertisers are well aware of the power of repetition, which is why the same commercials, songs, and advertisements are played ad nauseum. I am 37 years old as I write this book, and to this day I still remember that Dunkin' Donuts commercial on the East coast that played during the early 80's, which showed a man rising early every morning with the statement "It's time to make the donuts!" I have confused many a friend and lover when I have spent the night at their house and awakened in the morning singing "Time to make the donuts!" They look at me very confused and say, "I didn't know you were making donuts this morning, wow, what a treat." They are inevitably disappointed when I explain to them that donuts will not be forth-coming that particular morning, and that it is simply my cultural conditioning playing out.

Yes, I'm a joy to sleep with.

We are programmed from birth to accept certain behaviors, certain ideas, and certain beliefs all as part of our social conditioning. And yes, this is a vital function for us as humans, part of our socialization so that we can co-exist with a degree of relative, if not absolute harmony. Yet, many of the belief systems that we have been conditioned to accept, *especially* regarding our sexuality, are debilitating and harmful, and they are *external* suggestions that we have subconsciously accepted as our own.

These culturally-conditioned belief systems control how we think and feel about our own sexuality, preventing us from innocently exploring that aspect of our HUMANITY. This prevents us from knowing and understanding the truth of our own bodies, and our inherent connection to Divinity, which can be realized through our sensual awareness and sexual bliss.

We have been conditioned to fear our sexuality as women, by the social suggestion that bad things happen to "those" kind of girls. "Good girls don't, bad girls do." And who wants to be a bad girl? Cripes!

Bad girls at best get "knocked up" and live on the wrong side of the tracks in abject poverty, raising a child or two on their own, being social outcasts. At worst, they get raped and killed, and end up in a ditch somewhere, all for wearing a skirt that was too short, and having had too many lovers.

The Walt Disney Syndrome[21] encourages all little girls (and then teenage girls, and then grown women) to wish and dream for the handsome prince who will ride up in his shining armor, on his snowy white horse, give us the kiss of life, and awaken us to a glorious new world of happily ever after.

The underlying *suggestions* of these stories are:

> a) The girl has been living a life of relative suffering or boredom without out him,

> b) She is under an evil spell and is sleeping or "dormant" (sexually dormant),

> c) He is overcome with her beauty (pretty girls always win) and gives her the "kiss of life", bringing her to sexual, personal and emotional maturity.

> d) They ride off into the sunset, and live happily ever after, her arms wrapped lovingly around his waist, her Savior.

So what does this "fairytale" imply to my young female mind?

- *It implies* that my happiness as a woman is dependent

---

[21] I came up with the concept of The Walt Disney Syndrome while writing this book. Upon further research I discovered that a blogger named Lord Bayne also coined the term in 2010. I want to be clear that I was not influenced by his work in any way, but I would like to acknowledge that he used the terminology first. http://fubar.com/walt-disney-syndrome/b338517

upon finding the right man to "save me" and *life does not really begin* until that first kiss.

- *It implies* that my inner fulfillment as a woman lies in the hands of the perfect man, "my prince". He is also responsible for my sexual "discovery" and until he arrives, I will wait, and wish, and dream of someday.

   Ahhhhhh, someday...

And thus I wonder, *how many women* are still waiting for the "right man" in order to finally "find happiness"?

How many women found "prince charming" only to have him leave her for another woman 10 years and 2 kids down the road?

How many of us kissed man, after man, after man, desperately hoping, wishing and praying that he would finally be THE ONE, and we could finally be happy; the search would be over, life has now begun!

The point I am trying to make with all of this is that; from the time we are little girls, we are overtly and subtly conditioned through various types of cultural suggestion to believe that our **life happiness** and **sexual pleasure** lies in the hands of a man, our handsome prince, THE ONE.

Even the wildly popular Adult Erotica novel <u>50 Shades of Grey</u> follows the same pattern of the sexually awkward and essentially dormant young woman meets older, wealthy, and sexually powerful man, who takes her under his wing and proceeds to awaken her to her own sexual pleasure. She is enraptured and falls under his spell, devoted to this one man who has 'activated' her by giving her the 'kiss of life'. This pretty much reads like a Harlequin Romance novel in a modern day setting. A sexed-up version of Snow White and

Cinderella, including descriptions of what happens in the bedroom of the Big Castle, at the end of their sunset ride.

Women are discouraged from consciously exploring *their own* sexual pleasure, beyond a clitoral orgasm here and there, and many times not even that.

Many women have shared with me that they have never self-stimulated in any way, and felt very uncomfortable with the thought of doing so for themselves, as if giving themselves sexual pleasure would somehow 'take away' pleasure from their partner.

I remember thinking for most of my life that the inside of my vagina was "his territory", to be reserved for men, or "the right man" to explore. I was horrified at the thought of sticking something inside of me for my own pleasure, and did so with great reservation and quite tentatively at first, as if I would somehow damage the sanctity of my vagina by daring to venture into that territory on my own. This fear of owning, knowing, exploring, and understanding our own physical-sexual pleasure keeps us fragmented, helpless, weak, confused, and disempowered in life.

This fear of our own sexual *organs* keeps us disconnected from our intuition and the inherent knowing that arises from being deeply connected to our bodies and the visceral responses that they give us as guidance.

The body knows what it wants. There is a deep instinctive wisdom that we can tap into when we honor the information that it gives us in the form of visceral sensation.

Pleasure/happy=good

Pain/yucky=bad or dangerous.

It is that simple.

When we remain ignorant of the most basic understanding of how we *feel,* we relinquish control of not just our own pleasure, but our own clear wisdom and choice, into the hands of another person, usually our male partners. This is also disempowering for them, as they are now charged with the task of being responsible for our sexual satisfaction.

I believe The Walt Disney Syndrome contributes to sexual *dissatisfaction* for both men and women, (and partners of all genders) by encouraging unrealistic expectations for both parties. Women believe that the "perfect man" will know how to kiss her *perfectly,* and fulfill every sexual longing she has ever had (all of her sexual longings being fed to her through media, fairytales, and romance novels).

Men are aware of our expectation for them to know *exactly* what to do and "take the lead" sexually, as they receive their own cultural guidance about what good girls do and don't know in bed. They have to deal with the pressure of being responsible for our sexual pleasure, even though they receive absolutely NO education about how to *give* us pleasure, outside of mainstream porn. Internet and mainstream pornography are sadly not valid forms of sex education at this point, as the sexual activity portrayed is not demonstrative of authentic connection, emotional intimacy or *mutual* pleasure.

One of the real problems I see in this scenario is that because both men and women have this expectation that "he is just supposed to know", both people are afraid of *talking* to each other and communicating honestly about their sexual pleasure. I actually heard a so called "sex expert" giving sex advice to women encouraging them to "just moan a little louder when he does something you like, to let him know that he's on the right track." God forbid the woman should actually use *words* and volunteer any information such as "Yes! I really like that! That's really nice, please keep doing that!"

You would think that adults involved in sexual intimacy would not have to resort to playing charades in order to get their point across. I find it absurd that sex is the most physically intimate act that two people can engage in, and yet we are terrified of talking to each other and asking for what we want, or often even expressing what we enjoy. I have seen time and time again how the simple act of two people talking to each other about their pleasure, *during the act* of sexual pleasure, completely transformed their relationship, and built a deeper sense of emotional intimacy, which in turn led to a more consistent experience of *mutual* sexual satisfaction.

The Walt Disney Syndrome is absolutely devastating to sexual intimacy between partners, because it encourages each person to "play a role" and discourages the kind of intimate connection that only comes from emotional transparency.

Adding to all of that, we also continue to experience the influence of the 50's and 60's June Cleaver female stereotype, the woman who sacrifices everything for her family and asks for nothing in return - the golden woman who can bake a cake, clean a house, iron sheets, and have a martini ready for hubby when he gets home at the end of the day.

Our culture has a tendency to glorify self-sacrificing female role models who override their own needs for the sake of their families, friends, co-workers, and children. I am not suggesting that we become ruthlessly self-serving, I am suggesting a need for balance. We do not have to be entirely one or the other. We can create balance by connecting with and prioritizing our needs for self-pleasure as part of a healthy, balanced, and spiritually enriching lifestyle. The fact of the matter is that being disconnected from our own pleasure is actually detrimental, not just to our own health and well-being, but also to the people around us.

Being disconnected to the true source of pleasure within us leads to issues and behaviors such as:

a) Over-eating and binging
b) Anxiety, depression, and low self-esteem
c) Boredom and lack of joy and purpose
d) Low libido and limited sexual response
e) Being overly critical of self and/or others
f) Emotional outbursts, irritability, and arguments.
g) General unease, confusion, and dissatisfaction with life.
h) Co-dependence in relationships
i) Dysfunctional relationships and unhealthy relationship choices
j) Competition with other women

I believe the remedy to all of this lies in women reclaiming their right to sexual self-awareness, sexual expression, and most of all understanding their own sexual pleasure.

"Truth is that which does not contaminate you, but empowers you.

Therefore, there are degrees of truth, but, generically,

truth is that which can do no harm.

It cannot harm."

~ Gary Zukav ~

Self-Awareness Exercise ~

1) What do you think of The Walt Disney Syndrome? Do you see areas in which it has shown up in your life? If so, take a few minutes to connect with and write down, how and where it has influenced your life experience.

2) Also take a few moments to reflect upon how it has affected your connection to your sexuality. Have you felt, or do you feel discouraged from exploring your sexuality? Do you feel uncomfortable talking about your sexual pleasure with your partner?

3) Do you recognize in yourself any of the symptoms listed above that result from being disconnected from your self-pleasure

4) Take some time to write or share about anything else that comes up for you when thinking about The Walt Disney Syndrome

"The most common way people give up their power is by thinking they don't have any."

~ Alice Walker ~

Part Two ~

Creating A New Pleasure Paradigm

Chapter 12. Sensual Sovereignty ~ A New Paradigm of Pleasure

As I explained in Chapter 9, and will continue to show throughout this book, Pleasure is Medicine and understanding how to use all 4 forms of pleasure - physical, sexual, emotional and spiritual - is our path to inner freedom, personal empowerment, and soul expression.

The work of Naomi Wolf in her book <u>Vagina: A New Biography</u>[22] clearly demonstrates that a woman's relationship to her sexual pleasure is directly related to her feelings of self-confidence, competence, self-connection, purpose and passion, largely due to the chemicals released in the brain and body while *experiencing* that pleasure, as I mentioned in Chapter 5. Quite literally, the more empowered we are to feel pleasure, especially sexual and sensual pleasure, the happier, more motivated, and more inspired we are to live our dreams and contribute meaningfully to life.

It is by understanding our own unique experience of pleasure, and giving ourselves permission to explore and cultivate that pleasure, that we heal our hearts, minds, bodies, spirit, and eventually our entire planet. When we stop seeking our source of pleasure externally, and begin generating it internally, we become SELF-empowered, and our relationships cease being co-dependant. Instead, we experience '**Sensual Sovereignty**' which is a term I created.

---

[22] Naomi Wolf, Vagina: A New Biography, September 11th, 2012, Ecco U.K.

Sensual Sovereignty means ~

- *Being fully sensually and sexually self-expressed,*
- *Being mentally and emotionally free from social, cultural, and religious restrictions placed upon our sexual and sensual self-expression,*
- *Being deeply connected to our body, our pleasure, our sensual awareness, and inner Wisdom Guidance,*
- *Being emotionally, mentally and physically liberated from culturally conditioned sexual guilt, fear, and shame,*
- *Having the personal empowerment to freely explore, completely embrace, and fully enjoy our sensual-sexual experience,*
- *Expressing our sensuality and our sexuality in ways that feel enriching, satisfying, nourishing, and truly empowering, by being deeply connected to our internal source of satisfaction.*

When we fill up our own pleasure battery, we are able to give to life more fully, more authentically, and with more clarity, power and purpose.

By cultivating The Art of Self-Pleasure you will experience over time, and for the rest of your life (because healing from the inside out is a permanent state):

- Feeling deeply connected to the inherent passion, pleasure, and joy in life,
- Confidence in your self-expression,
- Feeling deeply connected to your inner Wisdom and Guidance,
- Clarity of Soul Purpose,
- Freedom from guilt, shame, and sexual confusion,
- Ongoing joyful exploration of your unique sensual expression,
- The ability to cultivate deep intimacy and enriching

relationships,

- Better physical health and emotional balance,
- Increased sexual sensation, orgasmic ability, and pleasure!
- Increased Life Energy, vitality, and connection to Life Essence,
- Inner peace of mind and contentment.

In **The New Pleasure Paradigm** we embrace pleasure as a powerful and positive element for personal growth, spiritual realization, and soul integration. We acknowledge the life-guidance that we receive from our bodies in the form of subtle sensations of pleasure or non-pleasure, trusting in the wisdom arising from within us. We experience that the more we honor that wisdom awareness, the clearer it becomes. We allow ourselves to become a conduit for the Divine Life current to flow through and out into Manifest Existence, transforming and healing as it goes.

The Art of Self-Pleasure ~ New Pleasure Paradigm ~"I am responsible for my own Sexual Satisfaction. Realizing my full pleasure potential is an inside job, and I am happy to SHARE that pleasure with my partner, without making him or her responsible for providing it."

My invitation ~

I invite you to begin using your internal guidance system and pleasure as a tool for self-connection and clarity, and vehicle for soul empowerment. We can create a new paradigm for life, that enhances not just own lives, but also the lives of everyone around us.

"A woman serves a man best when she has her joy above all other values."

~ Dr. Victor Baranco ~

Chapter 13. The 4 Principles of The Art of Self-Pleasure

The 4 Principles of The Art of Self-Pleasure are your foundation for life. They work together to create a solid basis for healing, personal transformation, and spiritual growth.

It is important to use at least 2 of these methods on an ongoing basis, in order to keep the ball rolling, and maintain momentum. Please keep in mind that each one of these methods is a powerful form of medicine, so there may be some days on which you resonate with one of the principles more than the others, because this is what your body/mind needs at that moment.

There may also be a day where you "feel full" and you don't want to do any of them. I encourage you to honor that. Please keep in mind that this is about cultivating pleasure, and sometimes doing absolutely "no thing" is the best medicine we can give to ourselves.

The Pleasure Program in Chapter 22 provides a framework for weaving these methods into your daily life, and gives recommendations for creating a solid, life-long practice for experiencing optimum results.

The 4 Principles of Self-Pleasure are:

1) *Movement* - The 5 Core Pelvic Movements™ and Feminine Emergence Dance

2) *Meditation* - Authentic Tantra® Meditations

3) *Self-Connection* - The Ocean Breath by Carla Tara, and Pleasure Journal (by Devi Ward)

4) *Self-Stimulation* - Authentic Tantra® and The Art of Self-Pleasure for Women

The outcome of practicing The 4 Principles of Self-Pleasure on a daily basis will be an increased sense of self-empowerment, self-satisfaction, passion, joy and of course pleasure in every area of your life.

Some Testimonials from the 21-day Pleasure Program August 2012 using The 4 Principles of Self-Pleasure

"Hello to all of you soul song shakers.... I was cleaning my home in preparation for heading to the Interior...and in between vacuuming...I was listening to tunes and practicing my figure 8's...half circles and energetic thrusts with glee...when finished...meditated on the colors and shapes...and enjoyed the best yet self pleasuring with the longest and most satisfying orgasm that I have ever experienced...thank you Devi!" K.F. ~ Vancouver, BC

"Thank you for sharing this magical gift! I feel so much more at peace and connected to the world around me, especially the beautiful pleasure awakening experiences available to me throughout the day." A.H ~ Vancouver, BC

"I am going to continue on with this methodology and practice regularly as the benefits really did start to come through a few weeks into it. The interesting aspect to this is that I set it up that I would do the dance portion and then have that lead into the self-pleasuring. This really brought about a new awareness for me. I am finding that my body is a bit more fluid in it's movement, which I like. I would always start the dance with the 5 core pelvic movements to get warmed up then put on a favorite song and really just have at her. A few times I danced with nothing on and I really enjoyed the freedom in that. It was also very sensual and I got to tease myself quite a bit. There has been a conscious awareness happening regarding my vaginal area. I have really been exploring the different points on my clitoris. Some areas are most definitely more sensitive than others. The other aspect has been playing around with the different types of pressure to apply once aroused. That has been one hell of an eye-opener. My god! Some of the orgasms have just been really intense...almost to the point where I almost can't bear to touch myself there anymore." N.P. ~ Vancouver, BC

"These methods really do make a difference. My pleasure is increasing noticeably, my body is more open, and my libido is through the roof!" K.T. ~ Ottawa, Ontario

"The real voyage of discovery consists not in seeing new landscapes, but in having new eyes."

~ Marcel Proust ~

Chapter 14. The Process of Pleasure

During this journey of sensual awakening and soul remembrance, it is important to keep in mind that all healing, growth and evolution take time. And make no mistake, by exploring your pleasure potential with these methods, you will evolve and grow into more of your *human* potential.

Personal transformation is not something that can be forced or rushed. Like a flower blossom opening petal by petal, it is important that you engage this process with a sense of ease, grace, and an unhurried mind. The journey into sensual awakening and empowerment is truly about that, the journey. *There is no static end goal to be achieved.* As long as we exist we will learn, evolve, and grow.

It is also important to keep in mind that we literally already are that which we seek, and this "process" is simply one of removing the veils or obscurations that prevent us from experiencing our already existing whole-ness. There literally is *nothing to be added.*

Even the methods themselves are simply tools to remove the "impurities" of mind and body. The mind and body themselves are already whole and complete, we are just going to do some house-cleaning, getting rid of thoughts, patterns, emotions, and ideas that no longer serve us, if indeed they ever did.

When I first began practicing Tibetan Tantric Meditations I found it a difficult and at times mentally exhausting practice, due to the elaborate visualizations included in some of the meditations. I initially found these internal visualizations to be challenging, because I was coming from the standpoint of having to *create* in my imagination something that was not already present. I spent quite a lot of energy attempting to 'conjure up' these visualizations, and *make* them appear.

Then a fellow practitioner suggested that I consider coming from the disposition of *allowing* that which I am attempting to imagine, to *already be present.* He suggested that the way the Universe works is that we are simply using our mental focus to become aware of that which *already* exists.

From this standpoint, you, me, we all are already sensually whole, sensually empowered, and deeply connected to the life within and all around us. We simply need to become more aware of that which already is. Quite literally, what we focus on grows, and as we become more aware of our sensual wholeness, we begin to experience that truth more and more.

Below are **3 golden keys** to keep in mind during your process of reawakening to your sensual wholeness:

Be gentle

Be diligent

Be compassionate

1. *Be gentle with the methods*

   We have a cultural tendency towards "pushing ourselves" beyond our limits.

   While there are times in which that driven energy can be useful, (like pushing through to a higher level of physical achievement), pushing too hard in your healing process can actually be detrimental to your results. The methods that I am sharing with you in this book are POWERFUL.

Some of them are Authentic Tibetan Tantric Instructions from a 2,600-year-old lineage. When done correctly over a period of time, they catalyze massive healing, transformation, clarity, and growth, and kind of like a homeopathic remedy, minute amounts over time can lead to exponential results. The Tibetan Lamas (teachers) frequently say "gently, slowly". There is no rush or hurry in getting from point A to point B, because there really is no point B.

I myself have been very hard and very driven, very YANG, and part of my healing process has been learning to be gentle with myself and yield to life, rather than try to attack it head-on. Feminine Essence is represented by the Yin, or yielding quality, and it is symbolized by water. Water is a yielding, receptive, yet powerful force. Overtime it will literally erode mountains. The United States has the Grand Canyon as a clear representation of how powerful the feminine yin element of water can be over time.

As we really have no idea what will arise to be "purified" or healed, and no idea of who and how we will be once that happens, it's important to keep in mind that pleasure, self-connection, and self-love are the only true goals and destination of our journey.

2. *Be diligent with the methods*

That being said, it is imperative that you actually apply the methods in order for them to work. Consistency is Key! You can buy an exercise video and watch it, but if you don't actually *do* it, there will be no change in your current experience. Or if you do it only sporadically, your results will be minimal, and very little new ground will be gained.

I give clear guidelines in the pleasure program in Chapter 22 for what I believe to be the most effective way to integrate this new "life style" and make it feasible to continue for the rest of your life if you wish.

Pleasure can often times be it's own reward, and my personal experience has been that if I enjoy not just the results of the practice, but also the practice itself, then I am much more inclined to do it on a regular basis. The methods associated with The Art of Self-Pleasure are fun and enjoyable, each in their own right. And the more they are engaged in, the more enjoyable they become, and the better and more definitive the results.

Another aspect of diligence to keep in mind is that you are undergoing a process of healing and removing what are called "blocks to bliss". Blocks to bliss are exactly that: obstacles in our mental, physical, and emotional bodies that prevent us from experiencing our true potential. When blocks arise we may feel physically or emotionally uncomfortable, agitated, annoyed, numb or over-sensitive.

It is important in these moments not to give up, especially if these experiences are arising during sexual self-stimulation. It means that some tension, stress, or trauma is releasing in the body/mind and making its way out to the surface. In these moments it's important to proceed, but with gentleness. Don't push through with force. Remember instead to breath and yield.

(Specific instructions for releasing sexual-emotional trauma during your self-stimulation are given in Chapter 19.)

If the sensation becomes unbearably intense, then yes, do stop for a period of time, but please try again as soon as possible. If you continually stop your healing process at the same place, it can actually reinforce that block over a period of time, and create an energy of resistance and fear. Keep in mind that on the other side of that uncomfortable experience is a whole new world of passion, pleasure, power, and joy. Sometimes it just takes a little diligence to get to the other side.

3. *Be compassionate with yourself*

It is of the utmost importance that you practice patience and compassion with yourself and your process. Again our culture can be very hard, yang, masculine, and driven. We are driven to succeed in life and the voice inside our own heads is often harsh and critical. We tend to project that voice into every area of our lives.

I myself am often surprised when other people don't judge me as harshly as I judge myself. Our life experiences program us to be overly critical of our perceived failures, and the desire to "get it right" can often distract us from being present in our bodies, and disconnect us from the subtle inner wisdom of our heart.

I encourage you to lavish upon yourself the love and tenderness that you would offer to a precious and much loved child or pet. Treat yourself with kindness, love, honor, dignity and respect. Celebrate your courage for embarking upon this journey into sensual wholeness. Allow the disenfranchised fragments of your soul to be welcomed home into the warm, loving embrace of your most authentic self.

Faith...

When you come to the edge of all the light you have,

and are about to step off into the darkness of the unknown,

faith is knowing one of two things will happen:

There will be something solid to stand on,

or you will be taught how to fly.

~ Patrick Overton ~

Self- Awareness Exercise ~

1) In your pleasure journal write down 3 criticisms that you have about yourself. They can be physical, emotional, or circumstantial; i.e. I am lazy, or I am too fat, etc.

2) Now take a few moments with each criticism and connect to how you feel inside when you give this message to yourself. Really get present to the emotional repercussions of your internal negative self-talk.

3) Now see if you can connect with the underlying desire, or "need" behind each criticism. What would be on the flipside of this self-criticism? What is it that you are yearning for instead?

4) Now see if there is any remedy that you can give yourself. Is there a strategy, or action that you can engage in, in order to create the experience that you desire?

For example:

1) My criticism is - My thighs are too big or I am too fat.

2) When I think this to myself I feel really sad and disappointed.

3) I have a desire for health, wellness, and beauty. I also have a deep need for self-acceptance and love.

4) The actions that I can take are exercising regularly to meet needs for health and wellness (NOT to punish myself for being "fat"), and asking my partner or a

friend to massage my thighs and verbally express how beautiful they are, exactly as they are.

You.Are.Amazing.

As. you. are.

Stronger than you know.

More beautiful than you think.

Worthier than you believe.

More loved than you can ever imagine.

Passionate about making a difference.

Fiery when protecting those you love.

Learning. Growing. Not alone.

Warm. Giving. Generous.

Quirky. Sexy. Funny. Smart.

Flawed. Whole. Scared. Brave.

And so, so, so.much.more.Be Strong. Be Confident. Be You.

~ Copyright: Tia Sparkles Singh, 2011~[23]

---

[23] http://www.yourlifeyourway.net/2011/10/10/75-most-empowering-inspirational-quotes-for-sassy-kickass-women/

Chapter 15. About The Methods

I have included in this book all of the methods that I have used, and continue to use, in order to cultivate presence, power, passion, and pleasure in my life. I believe that in order to effectively create change in our lives, we need to be regularly engaging in a *cause* for change.

For example, if I want to loose 10 pounds, it won't happen by my sitting on the couch wishing for it. I need to get up, off my butt, and DO something to make that happen. Put simply, I need to engage in a cause in order to get results.

When it comes to transforming our life experience, the desire to do so is absolutely fuel for the path, but desire alone is not enough. We must have a tool for transformation, and utilize that tool *on a regular basis*.

Albert Einstein himself stated, "A problem can not be solved at the same level it was created." Given that most of our cultural conditioning and wounding regarding sexuality occurred on a subconscious, almost subliminal, level, it is pretty much beyond our reach to go digging around for the source of it at the level of the intellect.

We need methods, tools, "power tools" if you will, that will work much deeper than our conscious or even subconscious mind. We need to work on an almost primal level, tapping into what we call in Tibetan Tantra "primordial wisdom awareness", which is a level of self- awareness beyond our ordinary, conscious thinking mind. In short, we need to access a level of wisdom held deep within our bodies, at the cellular level. But *how* do we gain access to that level of primordial wisdom awareness?

This is where Authentic Tantra™ comes in. The word 'Tantra' literally means, "to weave light and sound with form". The "Lights" are internal visualizations of specific colors, shapes, or images that tap into our primordial mind. The "Sounds" are specific mantras or "seed syllables" (also called Bija's) that resonate with a specific predetermined energetic vibration in the body. The "Form" is the body itself.

Visualizing this light, and toning these sounds causes the cells to *dance,* vibrate, resonate, and activate. The very *cells of your body* begin to release physical impurities and emotional imprints, which enable them to literally transform, heal and return to wholeness.

A beautiful visual demonstration of this process can be seen in the movie "What the Bleep do we know?" Though the movie does not refer to Tantra specifically, it does offer a clear visual depiction of how energy and vibration affect us on a cellular level. They also describe in this movie how our emotional experiences and self-critical internal dialogue play a large part in determining our physical state of health.

Dr. Masaru Emoto's book Messages From Water documents studies conducted with water crystals, which clearly demonstrate how the emotional vibrations associated with words (thoughts) change us on a cellular level- with positive life-affirming vibrations creating cellular structures of health and beauty, and life-defeating vibrations creating images of sickness, contortion, and disease[24].

Modern science has proven us to be more energetic mass than physical substance, and continuously confirms that thoughts are literally things, and energy goes where the mind focuses. It

---

[24] Dr. Masaru Emoto, Messages from Water, Vol. 1 (June 1999), Hado Publishing, ISBN 4-939098-00-1

stands to reason that if we are focusing one of the most powerful tools in the universe (the human mind) on primordial images designed to awaken us to our true interdependent connection to all of Life, we may begin to experience exactly that. Thus we begin accessing the inherent Divine Wisdom of our *Universal Nature.*

That's pretty empowered, don't cha think?

The ancient practices of Tibetan Tantra come directly from the Buddha, for the purpose of liberating all human beings from the suffering caused by being ignorant of our true nature, and the true nature of all life. Authentic Tantra™ is a style of sexual and non-sexual Tantra that weaves these ancient, lineage based methods with Taoist sexual yoga, and modern sex education.

Doing the practices included in this book does not make you a Buddhist. You do not have to believe in any of the theory associated with Tibetan Buddhism, or subscribe to any of its teachings. What I am sharing with you in this book are some basic and fundamental instructions that can be universally applied, regardless of your religious or spiritual beliefs.

The Secret Tibetan 5 Element Sexual Tantras were introduced to me in 2008 as a method for using human sexuality as a path to spiritual realization, and personal growth. This was very intriguing to me, as I had spent the previous 9 years as a Monk of the Ishaya order, practicing the Ishayas Ascension Mediation.

Though we did commit to 1 year of celibacy during our initial vows, ongoing celibacy was not a requirement of our monkhood. Sexuality was not frowned upon, but there was no special attention given to it, and using sexuality to attain any sort of realization was not mentioned. I don't believe anyone in the organization even had any idea that it could be done. Thus, though I was actively committed to developing a deeper connection and understanding of the spiritual nature of life, I remained ignorant of our true sexual potential as humans, and completely unaware of the direct relationship that sexuality plays in our personal and spiritual growth.

The direct relationship between sexuality and spirituality can be found in ancient Tibetan Tantric Teachings. It is explained like this: We have in our bodies a channel of energy called the central channel, uma channel or "sushumna nadi" in Sanskrit. This channel is the core of the Life Force in our bodies, and is where enlightened awareness resides within us. When the conscious mind comes in contact with this central channel, we experience profound bliss, void-ness, and "no mind". There is a moment of no thought, no sense of I, me, or egoic self. Our awareness is literally purified, and in this moment we are entirely free of cultural conditioning, programming, and the incessant dualistic chatter of our conscious, superficial minds.

It is to this central channel that most Yoga practices are geared to reach. Through years of focus, concentration, breath work, and difficult postures it is possible to begin accessing the wisdom residing in this central channel. Think of it as a golden palace that everyone is trying to gain admittance to, whether they are aware of it or not. All spiritual disciplines are geared towards accessing this central channel.

Now, the beauty of REAL Tantra is that it contains the original teachings on how to most easily and effectively access the "great palace" of the central channel. And guess what? The easiest, most effective way to access this area is through human, sexual pleasure. It is stated that at the moment of orgasm, the moving energies or "pranas" in the genitals brush the central channel, and we get a glimpse or "taste" of enlightenment. These teachings state that the human body is physiologically designed so that every orgasm, whether we are aware of it or not, is a direct experience of enlightened awareness.[25]

Think of that brief moment of orgasm, that split-second of pure bliss, pure ecstasy, and pure joy. There is no thought, no mind, just pure free awareness and bliss. Now what if you could extend that split-second to last for several seconds? What if you could rest in that bliss for longer and longer periods of time, lasting *several minutes* at a time? If a 2-second orgasm has beneficial effects upon brain and body chemistries, what do you think several minutes of orgasm would do for us in regards to physical health, emotional balance, and anti-aging abilities?

My Teacher, Lama Tashi Dundrup is 74 years old. He gets up every morning at 4 am to meditate for 2 hours before going to work. He runs a recycled appliance business on Kauai, Hawaii and works 5 sometimes 6 days a week, lifting, moving, repairing and delivering home appliances all over the 30 miles of inhabited island. He also runs a Shangpa Kagyu Dharma center with several thousand students, and regular evening dharma classes 2 nights a week, every week. He himself practices Authentic Tibetan Tantric Sexual Yoga with his Tantric consort. Can I mention again that he is 74?!

I personally began these practices in a place of deep emotional wounding and impaired physical health. I had devoted my life to spiritual practice, yet I had no understanding of how to integrate that "spiritual" awareness into physical reality, and

---

[25] Much of the teachings of Tibetan Buddhist sexual Tantra are kept in secret. and are not written down. These particular teachings on the function of human orgasm come directly from the Lamas themselves.

my every day life. I had no idea what a g-spot was, where it was located, or if I in fact even had one. I was disempowered in every area of my life, emotionally, physically, sexually, financially, even spiritually, for I was not connected to the essence of life and my purpose in it.

As I began practicing the methods of Authentic Tantra® both in and out of the bedroom, I began to heal. I began to awaken to aspects of myself that had been hidden and buried beneath deep layers of emotional-sexual wounding. By acknowledging my wounding, consciously feeling the pain of it, and allowing myself to see, hear, and experience it, I began to understand myself with greater clarity and a true, deep, abiding compassion. I regained access to my inner voice of wisdom, power, strength and purpose, and began to become responsible for my own joy and fulfillment in life.

As the wisdom was awakened within me, (and continues to be!) I experienced a deep sense of connection to the life inside of me, and in every other sentient being. At first I felt such surprise, because I hadn't realized how deeply disconnected I actually was, or how that disconnection is considered to be our "normal" state of existence.

Until I began to experience otherwise, I hadn't realized how desensitized, numb, and removed from life most of us are. I hadn't realized how the constant, incessant mental chatter, and emotional dysfunction that results from our ongoing inner conflict, creates these imperceptible layers, barriers, walls between ourselves and others, and prevents us from truly connecting to, and experiencing the life within and around us in every moment.

Each and every time I allowed myself to fully experience the secret treasure of pleasure that my body contained, I freed myself from the internal chains that held me bound to an

134

artificial sense of self and culturally-imposed standards of proprety.

As I rode the waves of orgasmic bliss inside my body, and literally flew in the sky of non-conceptual mind, my life changed. From the inside out, as a result of the methods that I engaged, my life changed - beyond my wildest dreams, and in ways I could have never imagined. I went from being unconsciously imprisoned, to blossoming open into limitless possibility, and *every day,* it continues, as these methods are a life-long practice.

Our lives are a work of art, continuing to unfold, continuing to blossom. If we have the right methods, we *cannot help* but achieve our ultimate realization. If we have the correct information, we *cannot help* but be awakened to the truth inside of us.

The process is inevitable, and the results are guaranteed. I am living proof, and my life is a testimony to the healing, health, pleasure and empowerment that lies within each and every one of us, once we gain access to the inherent wisdom awareness residing deep within.

"The way is not in the sky. The way is in the heart"

~ Buddha ~

* A note about Authentic Tantra® ~ There are a lot of people out there claiming that they know and practice Tantra, and yet a large percentage of these people have no idea what the word even literally means, or where it came from. This ignorance contributes to a large degree of misunderstanding about what Tantra actually is and how powerfully it can enhance and enrich our lives on every level. All Tantra is not the same, so Buyer- please beware!

Chapter 16. Principle of Self-Pleasure #1 ~ Movement

There is an innate sense of joy that I believe all human beings experience from the unrestrained self-expression, which comes through movement and dance. Dance is part of our primal human expression. From the time of the first cave-dwelling humans, to modern day native and aboriginal cultures, tribal celebrations often include dance as an integral part of their rituals.

Losing ourselves in the pleasure of movement allows our conscious thinking minds to disengage from our intellectual thought process, and reconnects us to the inherent wisdom of the body. Our culture is excessively intellectual, or as Lama Tashi says "top heavy". Dance is a fun, enjoyable, *pleasurable* method for getting out of our heads and into our bodies, into *present moment awareness*.

I believe having a regular dance and movement practice is essential to physical, emotional, and spiritual well-being for both men and women. We live in an angular, and at times rigid, emotionally disconnected world, and I believe one of the easiest ways to reconnect to our human essence, is through the unrestrained and joyful self-expression of celebratory dance.

Sensual dance is particularly healing for women, as it focuses on cultivating the more feminine qualities of movement such as fluidity, grace, beauty and of course, sensuality.

I have heard from many successful businesswomen, that they have felt they had to sacrifice their connection with their feminine essence, in order to pursue goals in business or career. As a result of their more "masculine" (or yang) mental and emotional disposition towards life, they noticed that their bodies had become somewhat tight and rigid, especially in the pelvic area, and they immediately recognized the soothing, healing effects that conscious sensual movement had upon their bodies, emotions, and mental disposition.

I developed Feminine Emergence Dance and The 5 Core Pelvic Movements™ as a way for women to easily, effectively, and enjoyably reconnect with that precious pearl of sacred sensuality lying deep within. The Art of Feminine Emergence Dance includes opening the body with **The 5 Core Pelvic Movements™** and Movement Patterns, and expanding the "sensual vocabulary" with The 5 Elements of Sensual Self-Expression.

The Physical Benefits

According to a recent study in the September issue of the Journal of Sexual Medicine, women who have the most open, fluid pelvic movements are the most easily orgasmic, and also tend to be multi-orgasmic. This would make sense, as our pelvic region is where sexual energy resides in the body, and if we are rigid and contracted in that area, chances are that energy is not circulating as well as it should be.

The study states that- "vaginally orgasmic women do not have blocked pelvic muscles. As a result, the walk is natural, with the natural unobstructed connection between leg, pelvis, and spine movement." It also states that having open, mobile and fluid pelvic movement may be a sign of good mental health, confidence, and a good sexual relationship. [26]

---

[26] Science Daily (Sep. 7, 2008)
http://www.sciencedaily.com/releases/2008/09/080904215626.htm

Having an open, unobstructed range of motion in the pelvis can also directly improve our physical and emotional health by allowing the energies in the lower half of our bodies to circulate more freely. Taoist Master Mantak Chia states: "The coccyx and sacrum are the gathering center of all major nerves and are closely related to the organs and glands. When they are open and connected, one feels balanced; when closed, one feels imprisoned."[27]

The sacral pump is also one of the primary ways the lower body lymph is circulated. When the sacral pump is locked or obstructed, the body's ability to effectively move toxins from that area is impeded, and this can negatively impact our physical health, as well as our ability to respond to sexual sensations.

Physical movement (a.k.a exercise) also releases positive, mood-enhancing chemicals in the body such as dopamine, endorphins, estrogen, and serotonin.

The 5 Core Pelvic Movements™ are designed to open the *full* range of motion in a woman's pelvic region, effectively working to liberate dormant/stagnant physical, sexual and emotional energy in and around the pelvis, genitals, and entire body.

The 5 Core pelvic movements are:

> **Thrusts**
>
> **Circles**
>
> **Half-Circles**

---

[27] Emergence of The Sensual Woman, pg 151. Saida Desilets, Jade Goddess Publishing 2006, Wailua, Hawaii

Figure 8's

Undulations

The 5 Core Pelvic Movements™ can be further broken down into isolated and expanded movement, and forward and backward movement. The openness experienced in the pelvic region is then translated to the upper body, naturally creating a pelvic - heart integration, and becoming The 5 Core Movement Patterns. Detailed instruction in **The 5 Core Pelvic Movements™** can be found on my Feminine Emergence DVD "Celebration!" or at any of my Sensual Awakening For Women Workshops or Sensual Empowerment Coaching Sessions.[28]

The Emotional Benefits

Some of the most exciting benefits of **The 5 Core Pelvic Movements™** and Sacred Erotic/Feminine Emergence Dance aren't just physically based. These methods also radically transform our emotional relationship with our bodies, and enhance confidence in our sensual self-expression.

Humans Beings tend to be creatures of habit, and as a result we have habitual movement patterns that are directly related to our mental and emotional life experience. How and what we think and feel about ourselves is directly expressed in our physical body. When we are feeling happy and entertaining positive thoughts, our bodies may feel light, fluid, and healthy. Conversely, when we are feeling depressed, or entertaining painful thought streams, our bodies may feel heavy and slow, and our resistance to illness or disease may be low. Again we encounter the concept that "thoughts are things", and not only

---

[28] Information about The 5 Core Pelvic Movements can be found at www.feminine-emergence.com

do they affect our external reality, they are also instrumental in how vibrantly alive we feel in our physical bodies.

The "rub" in all of this, (if you will), is that often the thoughts that most directly shape our reality, are the ones that we are completely unaware of. We are therefore usually manifesting from, and being motivated by, thought patterns that we can't consciously change, because we don't even know *that they are there*. This is where intuitive feeling and emotional imprinting comes in.

Most body workers know and agree that emotions are stored or "locked' in the body, and when our range of motion is limited by pain or discomfort in a certain area, chances are a stored emotion is responsible for - or contributing to - this block. Feminine Emergence Dance works *with* the body, using the naturally pleasurable sensation of sensual movement to gently explore these restricted areas in the pelvic region, (and the entire body), in order to uncover the unconscious emotional energies that may be trapped there. That energy is then effortlessly released through the joy and celebration of dance. It's that simple, easy, and incredibly effective.

This is a similar practice in many respects to using "dance as a healing art" as exemplified by Anna Halprin and The Tampala Institute.[29]

The 5 Elements of Sensual Self-Expression

Each of The 5 Core Pelvic Movements and Movement Patterns has an emotional resonance intrinsic to that gesture. Each **of The 5 Elements of Sensual Self-Expression** directly

---

[29] Anna Halprin, Dance As A Healing Art, LifeRhythm 2000, Mendicino, California
http://www.tamalpa.org/

correlates with one of The 5 Core Pelvic Movements and Movement patterns. These "Elements" are used as a vehicle for expanding our sensual vocabulary, and exploring our sensual self-expression with an attitude of joy, innocence, curiosity, and play.

The 5 Elements of Sensual Self-Expression are:

Sassy

Flirty

Graceful

Seductive

Nasty

There are many facets of feminine expression, and most of us are comfortable in one or 2 of these modes of expression. The 5 Elements of Sensual Expression give you an opportunity to 'try on' these different aspects and qualities of your feminine essence. By exploring beyond the boundaries of your current range of expression, you will discover facets of yourself that you have hidden, repressed, and disassociated from, usually due to hearing an external message implying that aspect of yourself was not appropriate in some way.

We tend to close down parts of ourselves without even being cognizant of doing so, and until we begin expanding beyond our current realm of expression, we will never rediscover those pieces of our soul that have been fragmented and disembodied. The 5 Elements of Sensual Expression give you a safe and supportive playing field to celebrate ALL forms of sensual self-expression, including the ones that our culture teaches us to fear.

The 5 Core Pelvic Movements and 5 Elements of Sensual Self-Expression are also directly related to the 5 elements of earth, water, fire, air and space. These movements can be used to activate and enrich the elemental energies of your body, supporting emotional and physical health through intentional movement and dance.

Below is the chart containing The 5 Core Pelvic Movements, 5 Elements of Sensual Self-Expression, and how they relate to the 5 elements of earth, water, fire, air and space.

Element - Movement - Erotic Expression

    Earth –Circles and ½ circles – Spicy/Sassy

    Water –Undulations– Seductive/Sensuous

    Fire - Thrusts –Nasty!

    Air –Figure 8's –Flirty

    Space –Whole Body Expansion/Openness – Grace

You can learn more about how The 5 Core Pelvic Movements relate to The 5 Elements of Sensual Self-Expression at my Feminine Emergence Dance Classes all over North America.[30]

"Free Your Hips and Your Mind Will Follow!"

~ Devi Ward ~

---

[30] www.deviwardtantra.com

How to use The Feminine Emergence DVD ~ "Celebration" ~

I recommend using the Feminine Emergence DVD in conjunction with this book, for ongoing cultivation of your "pleasure practice".

The 5 Core Pelvic Movements as demonstrated in the DVD are a *serious* core workout. You will notice some, if not all of the following results from doing them regularly (4 times/week):

- Strengthens the core muscles of the abdomen
- Whittles your waist
- Improves flexibility of the entire body
- Increases physical health, strength and vitality
- Improves feminine grace and fluidity
- Increases self-expression and joy
- Stimulates your sex drive
- Creates confidence in your sensual self-expression
- Increases orgasmic ability and creates connection with your sensual pleasure
- Tones your butt, hips, abs, and thighs.

Once you have watched the DVD a few times, and are familiar with the movement, use it to continue cultivating pelvic mobility and range of motion, but feel free to turn off the sound, and use your own music. At the end of the DVD, please feel free to add to or change the dance in order to give it your own personal flavor. I continue to use the DVD myself for maintaining core strength and pelvic flexibility.

Here are some testimonials of how Feminine Emergence Dance and The 5 Core Pelvic Movements™ have changed women's lives:

From Liz~ *"One of my deepest fears is that I am not a sexual being, and so I began the erotic dance classes to learn to trust in my own self expression with confidence. Through my classes with Devi the fear has begun to abate. Devi has shown me through dance and dance choreography how to open up to my own innate sensuality as a human being. Slowly, but surely my erotic dance expression is becoming unblocked. I am learning to trust in my own expression."*

From Deb~ *"Thank you, Devi, for the amazing expansion I have experienced in my body and psyche through dancing sexy with you. This is the first time I have experienced anyone, other than my lover, encouraging my sexual expression. It's easy and fun to keep practicing and my confidence grows along with my ability to groove the moves. Thank you for showing me more freedom."*

From Carrie~ *"Devi's Sacred Erotic Dance instruction is delicious internal alchemy. Devi's teachings nourish my body, cultivate my femininity, and revitalize my spirit. I savor the invitation in each class to soften, celebrate, and discover the places of beauty within my soul. The dance is a sacramental experience, allowing my heart to open and my movement to be guided from a place of inner calm. Sacred Erotic Dance is of such exquisite delicacy that if it speaks to you, it will enter your heart and change your life."*

Note- In 2005 I created The 5 Core Pelvic Movements™ and Sacred Erotic Dance™. Recently (2012) I changed the name to Feminine Emergence Dance because I discovered again and again that the word "erotic" was an emotional obstacle for many women.

Though some women were drawn to the idea of Sacred Erotic Dance, many more were fearful of exploring that aspect of themselves, and felt embarrassed at the idea of attending an Erotic Dance Class. My desire is to support as many women as possible in reconnecting with the sacredness inherent within their sensuality, and so I changed the name to in order to offer all women an invitation to explore this facet of them selves, in a way that is comfortable and non-threatening.

"Come to the edge", he said.

They said, "We are afraid".

"Come to the edge", he said.

They came.

He pushed them ...

and they flew. "

~ Guillauame Apollinaire ~

Chapter 17. Principle of Self-Pleasure #2 ~ Meditation

Having a daily meditation practice is absolutely essential for connecting to your inner wisdom, power, passion, and purpose in life. In order to clearly hear the subtle voice of wisdom inside we must be present, relaxed, and aware. Throughout the day the focus of our mind tends to be on the incessant chatter of our ongoing internal dialogue. All day long, and sometimes into the night, we are carrying on a discussion with ourselves about what we think and how we feel, in relationship to our life experiences, and human interactions.

"I like this, I don't like that. She said this, can you believe he did that? I can't believe I did that!" The commentary goes on and on, our internal critic continuously letting us know what is right, what is wrong, if we should be ashamed, if we should be proud, and what could/should be better.

Lama Rinchen, head of the Oahu Dharma Center often says before starting meditation: "From beginning-less time we have been following our thoughts. Now we will take a break and follow our breath."

The core purpose of meditation is to cultivate presence. But be aware, all meditation is not created equal. In this Era of New Age techniques, it can be difficult to discern what is actually worth doing, or if it is working effectively in our lives.

If your meditation is effective you will notice your life experience beginning to change for the better. Here are a few signposts that will indicate that your meditation *is* working, and that you are headed in the right direction.

1) You feel more relaxed inside, and have less "discursive" (negative) thought streams.
2) You feel more compassion for yourself and other human beings.
3) You feel more connected to all forms of life: human, insect, and animal.
4) Your intuition and sense of knowing becomes stronger, clearer, and more accurate.
5) You begin to "just know" how to do things, and begin to demonstrate a greater aptitude of your current skill-set.
6) Your overall health and resistance to disease improves. (I know many Authentic Tantra® meditators who completely stop contracting colds and never get the flu)
7) You begin to experience an inner sense of contentment and unexplained joy
8) Your overall happiness increases and beneficial life circumstances arise

These signposts are not to be looked for all at once. Meditation is a life-long practice, and though the methods included in this book are powerful, some results do take time. How much time depends entirely upon your "karma" and is entirely unique to each person. That being said, many people notice results such as peace of mind and quieting of thought streams almost immediately.

"You must learn to be still in the midst of activity and to be vibrantly alive in repose."

~ Indira Ghandi~

The Meditations ~

The first 2 of the following meditations are used by Tantric Buddhist practitioners worldwide, and are the foundational practices for all of the higher Tibetan "Tantra Yogas".

The first practice is to follow and count 21 breaths. This particular method has been used for the last 2,600 years as a tool for cultivating relaxed awareness with focus. This practice comes straight from the Buddha Shakyamuni (THE Buddha) down through 2,600 years of unbroken lineage, to Lama Tashi Dundrup, from me, to you.

Many people ask why we count the breath, and not just "watch" or witness the breath, and the reason can be found in the intention. The intention is to *cultivate presence*. It is easy to simply witness the breath, with no activity of counting, and think that we are actually remaining present. The reality is, that the mind is simply free to roam, and often wanders without us even being aware of it. When we give the mind the task of not only witnessing the breath, but also counting each and every breath, we notice how easy it is to "get lost in thought" and lose our place in the count. The object is to remain so focused and aware, that no matter what is going on inside our minds, (and eventually our external experience), that we never lose our focus and misplace our count.

It is said in the texts that "If you cannot follow 21 breaths in a row, the horse is riding the rider", meaning your mind is out of control, and has very little focus or discipline. What's the key to actualizing our desires in life? One-pointed focus on our goal, and Authentic Tantra® Meditations are a highly effective method for cultivating that laser-like focus.

The First Practice ~

1) Observe the 5 points of meditation which are
     a. Spine straight,
     b. Head with chin tilted slightly downwards to align the chakras[31] along the central channel,
     c. Tongue on the roof of the mouth,
     d. Hands in a comfortable position,
     e. Eyes doing a soft-gaze 2-4 feet in front.

(In Tantra we meditate with the eyes *slightly open* in order to integrate our internal experience with our external world. The saying is "inside, outside, same".)

2) Focus is at the nose. While inhaling and exhaling through the nose, watch the natural rhythm of your breath.

3) Now count 21 breaths. The count is at the end of each exhalation. One inhalation, one exhalation together equals one breath.

4) Count from 1-21 and then pause.

If you lose your place anytime during this practice, stop and start over again! This prevents us from developing bad meditation habits. Remember the object here us to cultivate

---

[31] Chakra simply means "wheel". Chakras are energy centers in the body, aligned along the central channel, and which correspond to all of our major organs.

presence. If you lose your count, you have lost your focus, so simply begin again.

The Second Practice ~

The 2ⁿᵈ meditation practice is called "color breathing", and this is an authentic Tibetan Tantric Meditation used for thousands of years to purify the mind, and reveal our true, limitless awareness. As I have said in previous chapters, Tantra literally means "to weave light and sound with form", and this particular meditation gives you a clear experience of exactly how that is done.

This meditation is to be done directly after counting 21 breaths.

1) After 21 breaths, stop counting and follow a few breaths without counting

2) Now, upon inhalation color the in-breath white, or see it as white light coming in through the nose.

Pause; change the air to red in color inside the body.

Exhale blue-light through the nose.

Repeat this for 3 breaths.

3) Next, while inhaling white light, think: "OM".

Change to red inside and think: "AH".

Exhale blue light and think: "HUNG" (sounds like a cross between hoong and hum).

Repeat for 3 breaths.

4) Lastly, while inhaling white light, think: "OM, positive

thought".

Change to red inside and think: "AH, positive speech".

Exhale blue light and think: "HUNG, wisdom in action".

Repeat for 3 breaths.

5) Finish by continuing to follow your breath, but instead of colored light, just breathe clear light in and out, as long as you want. No need for counting, just stay relaxed and aware.

The Third Practice ~

The 3rd meditation practice is the "fire element meditation." This meditation practice is unique to our school (Authentic Tantra.com), as we are the only school for Sexual Tantra currently offering the Secret Tibetan 5 Element Practices. This particular version of fire element meditation was directly inspired by Lama Tashi's guidance for using the fire element Tantric practices with women, during my Feminine Emergence Dance classes in Kauai, Hawaii.

The fire element is seated in the pelvis, inside the body, in front of the spine, and behind the pubic bone, along the central channel. The color is red, the shape is a 3 dimensional red pyramid, and its seed syllable (or Bija in Sanskrit) is RAM.

The fire element rules the sexual system, the muscular structure, and all of the electrical impulses in the body. It has the activity of magnetizing or attracting, and is the antidote (or medicine) for the emotional suffering of attachment.

By using this meditation on a daily basis, as well as integrating it into your sexual self-pleasuring as described in Chapter 19, you will begin to break up energetic, as well as physical obstacles in your sexual system. You will also be activating, healing, and enriching the fire element in your body, and will reap the rewards of having this elemental energy working more effectively in your life.

Interestingly, many of our female Tantra students who were single when they took our classes, found that they began to attract more potential partners after a period of cultivating their sexuality, and meditating regularly with the fire element. I find it sadly amusing (but understandable) that so many women want to wait until they have a partner to begin cultivating their sexuality, when really, it works the other way around!

They key to lasting happiness is to be found from the inside out, not outside in. By regularly engaging the fire element meditation, you will begin "breaking up" some of your core conditioning regarding relationships, and remove obstacles to intimacy and sexual connection that you weren't even aware of. Many women have found that within a relatively short period of time, their entire view of relationship and intimate connection transforms, becoming more empowered and healthy, with less co-dependence, and more emotional freedom and self-satisfaction. They naturally draw to themselves partners who reflect their new state, and are interested in cultivating a more meaningful intimate connection.

Always remember, "inside, outside, same", so as we transform and heal our internal experience, our external experience will naturally and inevitably reflect that growth.

This practice is to be done directly after the Tantric Color Breathing as described above.

1) Complete 21 breaths and Tantric Color Breathing as already instructed.

2) Begin by visualizing a red point of light at the heart center, inside the body, just in front of the spine. See the point grow to a 3-dimensional red sphere of light, about the size of a large grape.

3) See this red sphere of light travel down the center of the body (or central channel), and come to rest in the pelvis.

4) See the red sphere change to a red pyramid, 3 dimensional, with the point upwards.

5) In glowing red light, see the letters RAM in the pyramid, and chant RAM 21 or more times to yourself internally, and/or externally to affect environment. (You will have the most powerful effects from chanting this "mantra" out loud, as it affects not only the fire element internally, but in your external environment as well)

6) Visualize/See the 3-dimensional red pyramid change back into a 3-dimensional red sphere, travel up the central channel, back to the heart center.

7) Visualize the red sphere slowly shrinking to a red pinpoint of light, and then disappear into space.

8) Relax and allow the mind to rest in stillness.

Suggestions for how often and when to use these meditations are given in Chapters 19 and 22. You can certainly use it more often if you like, but I do not suggest using it less. Remember, consistency is key, so if you are not able to meditate everyday, or are not so inclined, having a minimum practice of 3-4 days a week will keep the beneficial process moving forward.

A note about your experience - When you first begin your

meditation practice, and at alternate times throughout, you may find yourself having LOTS of thoughts, almost as if you are having more thoughts now than when you began. That is not actually the case. Through the practice of meditation you are cultivating a deeper level of awareness, and are simply becoming conscious of the thoughts that you were previously unaware of. The analogy in the texts is this: At first when you begin your meditation practice the thoughts may seem overwhelming, like a waterfall or deluge of thinking and thought streams. Then as you continue your practice, the waterfall slows to a stream, and then a slow trickle. Then you become aware of the great expanse of mind, like the ocean. Then you dive into the depths of the ocean and swim.

Commentary from Lama Tashi Dundrup on this Chapter-

"Ordinary thinking develops into extraordinary thinking develops into no thinking at all. Spontaneity occurs naturally in one's body, speech and mind. This is of great benefit to all other sentient beings and to our environment mother earth. i.e. non self, voidness, awareness, clarity, bliss, mahamudra, dzogchen, the great perfection, etc. etc. etc."

Chapter 18. Principle of Self-Pleasure #3 ~ Self-Connection

The need for self-connection is a core, fundamental, human need that is often overlooked in our very busy, and somewhat superficial modern lives. In my opinion, self-connection is the "pot of gold" that we are all searching for in life: *to know the voice of your own heart with such depth and certainty, that every movement you make in life is the purest, most refined expression of your soul.* This kind of pure, undiluted, completely uncontrived self-expression is what we all crave as human beings, and only comes from having a clear, deep and unobstructed connection to our internal source of wisdom.

Unfortunately, given the training that we receive (or don't receive) as children, this sort of self-connection is easier talked about than experienced. When I began my spiritual journey at the ripe old age of 23, I remember frequently hearing the phrase "the answer lies inside" and "listen to your heart". Yes! I would think. That would be AWESOME! I just don't know how to do that. HOW do I get inside to listen? How do I hear the voice of my own heart over the racket in my head?

Well, that would require a tool for cutting through all of that surface-level mental chatter. Almost every form of growth in the human realm requires a tool. For example, if you want to cultivate (or grow) your vegetable garden, you need shovels, rakes, hoes, etc.

You need some sort of instrument to *get in there,* and dig around, pull up weeds, make rows… you get the picture.

So in the case of cultivating the garden of our hearts so to speak, we need a tool or a method that will *connect* us from the surface level of the mind, to the inherent wisdom residing within the body. We can't just expect to go from point A to point X, Y & Z with no clear method, tool, or vehicle to take us there.

All of The 4 Principles of Self-Pleasure will absolutely support you in experiencing a deeper, clearer understanding of your own heart, body, mind, and help you to hear the true and undiluted song of your soul with unmistakable certainty. Actively engaging in each of the 4 Principles is a *cause*, and the result will be:

- Inner clarity
- Soul connection
- Inner peace and a sense of ease
- Internal Joy
- Fearlessness and freedom of expression
- Increase in sensual pleasure
- Increase in emotional connection
- Improved relationships
- Inner empowerment

While writing this book I test-ran a 21-day pleasure program that included participants actively engaging all 4 Self-Pleasure Principles on a daily/weekly basis. They reported feeling more alive, more connected, more joyful, increased energy, more sexual pleasure, "the best orgasms of their lives", deeper intimacy with their partners, and a whole host of other life-enhancements.

Some quotes from participants were included in Chapter 15.

In addition to the exercises that specifically address the principles of Movement, Meditation, and Self-Stimulation, I have included two exercises that I regularly engage in to deepen Self-Awareness and Self-Connection.

The first method for Self-Connection again works with your breath. As I have stated throughout this book, our breath is *literally* a gateway to the present moment. Our breath bridges the gap between the heart and intellect, by redirecting our awareness into our physical bodies. Simply placing your focus *on your breath* gets you 'out of your head', and present in *your body*, an experience that many people are unconsciously trying to avoid.

Aside from the Tibetan Tantric Meditations that I described in the previous section, one of my favorite tools for creating present, body-centered awareness is The Ocean Breath.

"Within you lies the simple silence. Be quiet and listen..."

~ Author Unknown ~

Self-Connection Exercise #1 ~ The Ocean Breath

The Ocean Breath is a style of Tantric Breathing developed by Carla Tara, one of my Tantric Instructors. She developed this style of breathing for the purpose of healing and releasing emotional/sexual trauma stored in the cellular tissue of the physical body, as well as expanding and deepening the orgasmic experience.

Unlike many Yogic or Tantric Breathing styles, the ocean breath is a very feminine, or "yin" style of breathing. Many people find this breath difficult because it requires a large degree of emotional vulnerability, and present body-centered awareness in order to perform correctly.

In this book, I have included the version of The Ocean Breath as taught by Authentic Tantra®, and thus it may vary from what you would learn from Carla Tara herself. For understanding the true depth and power of this particular Tantric technique, I recommend her book <u>The Secrets of The Ocean Breath</u>™.

You will begin The Ocean Breath by lying on your back with your eyes closed, *and hands covering your belly*. This is a crucial element to doing the ocean breath properly, as it is important for your conscious mind to connect with the natural rise and fall of your belly, as you complete each inhalation and exhalation.

The next part in the process is to begin breathing with an open mouth. Most of the breathing that we do in our modern lives is very shallow, nasal, "rabbit breathing" that uses only *one tenth* of our actual lung capacity. This short, shallow style of breathing is usually a result of too much mental activity, and signals a lack of body-centered awareness. One of the key things that you may notice as you become more present in and attuned to your body, is that your breathing pattern will become much slower, much deeper, and much less frantic. You will no longer be locked in that fight or flight response pattern that so many of us are habitually engaging in.

Your mouth will need to be WIDE open for this breath, not just lips slightly parted.

1) We generally teach this style of breathing by having students take their first two fingers, (pointer and middle), turn them sideways, and place them in their open mouths, kind of like a dog with a stick in it's mouth. (See fig.1)

2) Now relax your jaw to a comfortable position around your fingers.

3) Take your fingers away, but leave your mouth open *exactly as wide as you just had it*, when your fingers were inserted. (See fig.2)

4) Continue to inhale and exhale through your open mouth, without closing it, even a little bit.

> ** Note-* The mistake that most people make is to unconsciously close their mouths while inhaling through the nose, and then open it again just slightly for the exhalation. Because we are not accustomed to breathing with open mouths, having the mouth even just slightly opened can feel as though we are doing the breath correctly, but this is not so! When you are initially learning this breath, I invite you to regularly

check the width of your exposure by using the two-finger method that I described above.

5) The last part of the ocean breath is to use sound. Again we are unaccustomed to consciously making non-verbal sounds in our culture, though we make plenty of unconscious non-verbal sounds on a regular basis! The sound that you are going to make with this breath is "hAAAAHHHHhhhhhhhhh", and it is a crucial aspect of experiencing the full effect of this particular breathing method. Continue breathing with a wide open, but relaxed jaw, and on every exhalation, allow the sound "Ahhhh" to "roll out" like an ocean wave meeting the shore.

A bit about the sound - In Tantric Buddhism, AH is the primordial sound from which all other sounds arise. The sound AH is also attributed to the throat chakra in some Tantric Practices. Making that sound has a similar effect to the practice of "sound healing", as it causes the throat chakra to begin vibrating. This vibration causes the throat chakra to activate and begin purging itself of blocks and obstructions that may be preventing us from speaking our truth in life. We are conditioned as children to NOT speak our truth, due to the embarrassment that can cause many adults who have learned to repress their authentic expression. We are encouraged to shut down our self-expression (sometimes forcibly), to avoid making other people uncomfortable.

We as individuals, and therefore as a culture, carry a LOT of baggage in our throat center. The Ocean Breath is a fantastic method for easily and effectively clearing this baggage out, and supporting us in reclaiming the internal voice of our hearts, as well as freeing up our ability to express ourselves authentically and powerfully.

"Seek always for the answers within. Be not influenced by those around you -by their thoughts or their words."

~ Eileen Caddy ~

Figure 1.

Figure 2.

Self-Connection Exercise #2 ~ The Pleasure Journal

Another one of my favorite methods of connecting with the voice of my own heart is through journaling. The process of writing can give us access to deeper levels of self-awareness by stimulating different areas of the brain. Writing Therapy is widely used these days to support people in processing traumatic events in their past, and facilitate emotional healing.

Most people are familiar with the idea of a gratitude journal, a nightly ritual where you write 5 things for which you are grateful. What you focus on grows, and the idea behind the gratitude journal is – if we focus on the abundance, joy, and prosperity already present in life, chances are we will naturally attract more of that to ourselves.

The Pleasure Journal follows a similar principle. Rather than have you get all geared up and focused on all the many ways in which you are going to take charge and start creating more pleasure in your life, I am interested in having you focus on the pleasure and enjoyment in life that you are *already* experiencing.

There are a multitude of ways in which our needs for sensory, sensual, emotional, and spiritual pleasure are being met *right now,* and I feel it is of the utmost importance to begin with that which is already present, before attempting to create more.

As I have said, our propensity in life is to "make it happen" and "get it done" which is entirely appropriate in some instances, but certainly not all. This very yang-driven (masculine) approach to life can actually prevent us from connecting with the softer, more receptive qualities within us, and may impede our ability to hear our own subtle, internal guidance.

The Pleasure Journal is a way of cultivating appreciation and awareness of the pleasure that is already present for us in our lives. Then from that place of inner fullness, we can look to creating more.

The exercises in this book have you focusing on cultivating awareness of the pleasure already existing in your life. Please use them as guidelines and do not feel as though you have to adhere to them exactly every time you journal. For example, if, as part of your journaling process, you discover some previously unrecognized trauma, and would like to give voice to that as well during your writing, then please do. Remember this is about cultivating YOUR personal pleasure program. I can only give you guidelines about how to begin the process. It is your Soul-Song that is being awakened, so please feel free to invent and adlib as you see fit. This will contribute to the blossoming of your inner voice, and the full embodiment of your soul-expression.

Creating Your Pleasure Journal

To begin your Pleasure Journal, I invite you to let your heart roam, and connect with the vibrational *essence* of pleasure, and the *possibility* of it in your life.

Pleasure Journal Exercise #1

Step 1. On the first page of your pleasure journal write between 10-20 different ways in which your needs for pleasure are currently being met, or ways in which you would enjoy having them met. This is your opportunity to celebrate the pleasure that already is, and become aware of creating *even more* in your life. I suggest creating one section that lists pleasures that currently are being met in your life already, and another section for those pleasures you look forward to experiencing.

You are certainly welcome to add to this list as you go, so leave plenty of room to grow!

Step 2. Now at your leisure, it doesn't have to be done all at once, start to identify which of The 4 Forms of Pleasure each listed item has met, or will meet. There can and will be overlaps, as very rarely are we experiencing only **one** of those forms of pleasure at a time. The ultimate human experience is having 3 or more forms of pleasure met at the same time. That is definitely a 10!

Pleasure Journal Exercise # 2

The next part of the self-connection process is keeping a daily pleasure journal. I personally find my life experience to be truly enhanced by taking time each day to appreciate the simple pleasures in life that are so easily overlooked. Your **daily pleasure journal** is a fantastic way to cultivate awareness of what is meeting your needs for pleasure in each and every moment. Remember, what we focus on grows, so if we are focusing on pleasure, we will see more and more of it showing up in our lives. Calling it in, so to speak!

I usually recommend doing your daily 'pleasure journaling' in the evening before bed, as a beautiful way to reflect upon your day, and connect with the little bits of beauty that were experienced throughout. This being said, you are welcome to use your pleasure journal at anytime that feels most appropriate for you, be it morning, afternoon, or evening.

The exercise is quite simple. On a daily basis, write down the answers to each of these questions in your journal:

1) What are some things that you appreciate about your life? Name at least 1-3 things.

2) What are some things that you appreciate about yourself? These can be physical, mental, emotional, qualities, etc. Name at least 1-3 things.

3) What are some ways in which your need for pleasure was met today? Name at least 1-3 ways. For an extra bonus, you can also name which of The 4 Forms of Pleasure were being met.

4) Did any experience today qualify as a 10? If so, what was it? Again, connect with which of The 4 Forms of Pleasure were being met for you during this experience for some extra depth and self-discovery.

5) Name at least 1 thing that you would like to do tomorrow to meet your need for pleasure.

Many experiences in life are enhanced when we share them, and this absolutely applies to pleasure. We have a saying in Authentic Tantra®- "Love is desiring happiness and pleasure for others", which means that love is something we do, not just something we feel inside. It is an expression of Life Energy and a contribution to Life itself.

So, adding to all that has come above, is the next step-

6) Name one way in which you met the need for

pleasure for someone else, or would like to meet that need for someone else.

Often times we contribute to the happiness of others without us even knowing. But sometimes, it can be very obvious, and I encourage you to make note of and celebrate that.

Also, at some point you may decide to make a daily challenge out of consciously contributing to other people's pleasure and happiness. As your pleasure battery is filled up from the inside out, you may naturally find your desire to share that experience with others arise with greater clarity.

"Your own words are the bricks and mortar of the dreams you want to realize. Your words are the greatest power you have.

The words you choose and the use establish the life your experience."

~ Sonia Croquette ~

Chapter 19. Principle of Self-Pleasure #4 ~The Art Of Self-Pleasure for Women

The 4th Principle of Self-Pleasure is Self-Stimulation, a.k.a The Art of Self-Pleasure. Self-Stimulation is a subject that makes many women feel quite uncomfortable. If the topic should ever come up, most women usually giggle nervously, and try to avoid eye contact with the other people in the room. Before my sexual healing through Authentic Tantra®, I myself would NEVER in a million years admit that I masturbated. And I never, ever, ever put anything inside my vagina. Before I was sexually active, it was for fear of breaking my hymen and "ruining" myself. After I was sexually active, it was because I was just simply terrified of putting anything "in *there*".

I don't know if I was afraid that it would hurt, or if it was just a general fear of all things vaginal. I do remember having a sense that the internal workings of my vagina were "a man's territory" and all of the sexual erotica that I had read by that point confirmed that supposition.

Self-Stimulation or 'The Art of Self-Pleasure' is a subject that is very near and dear to my heart, because it has been a place of such deep fear, ignorance, and wounding for me personally, and for about 95% of the women that I have encountered. Because it has been a place of such deep *disconnection*, as my relationship to sexual pleasure has healed, it has become a source of tremendous self-connection, self-empowerment, and self-love. By giving myself permission to do more than just masturbate, but to actually *explore* and *cultivate* my sensual-sexual pleasure, I feel as though I have reclaimed my own body.

As women, our orientation to orgasm tends to be modeled after a male ejaculatory orgasm, which generally takes about 2-7 minutes, is genitally localized, and climactic, meaning he comes and he's done, show's over.

But a female orgasm can be quite different from a male ejaculatory orgasm[32] when we are engaging the entirety of our sexual pleasure organ. Due to the culturally conditioned 'fear' of all things vaginal, I find that many women tend to be very clitorally focused when they masturbate, ignoring not just the depths of their vaginas, but also their entire bodies, whereas **The Art of Self-Pleasure** is a full contact sport.

I have been teaching women The Art of Self-Pleasure since 2009. What I teach is what I have discovered in my own personal journey of reclaiming my **sensual sovereignty**. You will not find these methods in any other book. They are the 'original choreography' of yours truly, and the "moves" have been developed carefully overtime. The purpose (or motivation) behind the methods described in this book is to awaken the full orgasmic potential of every woman by releasing the sexual/emotional wounding still present in the vagina. I believe this hidden wounding prevents a large percentage of women from experiencing not just their full sexual potential, but also their full *human* potential, as the two are intricately intertwined.

When it comes to sexual healing and personal transformation, you can talk about it until you are blue in the face, but nothing is going to actually happen until you get in there and start touching your vagina. Though regular clitoral stimulation is *awesome,* I do not believe that clitoral stimulation alone is

---

[32] Men are completely capable of multiple *non-ejaculatory* orgasms, using semen retention methods.
www.authentictantra.com

sufficient for truly liberating our bodies and minds from culturally-conditioned sexual repression, and reclaiming our sensual sovereignty.

Recent scientific research seems to agree. A study done in 2011 by female sexuality pioneers Drs. Barry Komisaruk and Beverly Whipple discovered that when different areas inside the vagina were stimulated, different areas of the brain were activated, catalyzing a variety of complex emotional and chemical responses in the body.[33] My personal experiences as a Tantric practitioner and educator have continued to demonstrate that much of the subconscious sexual-emotional tension and trauma that we hold in our bodies is 'stored' deep within the vaginal tissue, and it is only through consciously touching and pleasuring the whole vagina, that those stagnant energies are released, and we are truly psychologically and emotionally liberated.

This is because emotional-sexual trauma does not heal entirely on the level of the intellect. It heals on a cellular level, through touch, breath and awareness. Our path to sexual empowerment as women lies in reclaiming the depths of pleasure in our *entire* vaginas, and becoming confident and comfortable with our own sexual touch. Until we feel completely comfortable, relaxed and connected with our own sexual touch, we will not feel fully empowered in our sexuality. I have released layers and layers of socially suggested sexual guilt and shame, and reclaimed an inner sense of confidence and self-acceptance by allowing myself to pleasure my *entire* vulva and vagina, not just my happy little clitoris.

In Chapter 5, I mention the studies cited by Naomi Wolf that

---

[33] Naomi Wolf guardian.co.uk, Saturday 8 September 2012- The brain science of the vagina heralds a new sexual revolution & Vagina: A New Biography, September 11, 2012;

showed that when a woman thinks about enjoyable sex, and feels knowledgeable about her body and in control of her own sexuality, she exhibits more confidence, trust in her own judgment, motivation, personal drive, and feels blissful (happy), as a result of the dopamine and other chemicals that are released from this inner sense of sexual empowerment. Science confirms what I, and many other women have experienced, that the more empowered we feel about our own sexual pleasure, the more empowered, confident and capable we feel in other areas of our lives.

Yet, recent statistics show that as many as 40-70% of women have never had a vaginal orgasm, and as many as 10-15% of women never orgasm under *any* circumstances. [34] We as women are capable of *at least* 11 different kinds of orgasm, including multiple whole body orgasms. If this is our true pleasure potential, then why is it that so many of us have barely scratched the surface of our orgasmic ability?

There are 3 major reasons for this as I see it. They are:

1) **Lack of Education**
2) **Lack of Awareness**
3) **Lack of Sensation**

Reason #1 ~ Lack of Education - According to Sherri Winston, Author of <u>Women's Anatomy of Arousal,</u> "Women have an entire network of highly erogenous erectile tissue surrounding the vagina, creating an entire internal structure of

---

[34] Susan Donaldson James Sept. 4, 2009
http://abcnews.go.com/Health/ReproductiveHealth/sex-study-female-orgasm-eludes-majority-women/story

interlocking sexual "pleasure parts".[35] Recent studies confirm that women have as much erectile tissue inside our sexual pleasure organs, as a man does in his penis. Ours is just internal.

Because we have such an extensive network of erectile tissue, it takes us awhile to become fully engorged, anywhere from 20-45 minutes! This network of highly pleasurable erectile tissue makes up our entire "sexual pleasure system", and yet with the average duration of sexual penetration only lasting between 2-7 minutes, this doesn't give us a whole lot of time for that tissue to engorge, and for our bodies to become fully responsive to sexual stimulation.

Because most of us have been unaware (or uneducated) about the way a woman's body is actually designed, we have been unable to take into account these basic, physiologically-based sexual responses. As Sheri Winston says "We have been unable to play our instrument the way in which it was truly designed to be played."

If we have no understanding of how our "sexual pleasure organs" really work, we certainly have very little impetus to explore their "pleasure potential". Instead we think that a) whatever we have currently experienced is the extent of our ability, and /or b) there must be something wrong or defective with us because we aren't having super orgasmic experiences like the women we see in porn, or read about in 50 Shades of Grey.

Becoming educated about our bodies and our sexual pleasure potential is the first step in reclaiming our **sensual sovereignty**

---

[35] Sheri Winston, Women's Anatomy of Arousal: Secret Maps to Buried Pleasure, September 1, 2009

as women.

Reason #2 ~ Lack of awareness - This could tie into the reasons stated above, lack of awareness of our true potential, but in this case I am meaning it in a more literal sense, as in lack of "present moment awareness."

One of the largest detractors of experiencing our full orgasmic pleasure potential is the inability to remain present, relaxed, aware and focused in the moment. Our habit in life is to be up 'in our heads', following our conflicting thought patterns, and we tend to have very little to- no connection with our bodies, especially the lower extremities. We must inhabit the body fully and entirely to begin accessing all of the magic and wisdom that it has to offer us. This is why the movement, meditation, and Ocean Breath are such vital ingredients in your recipe for sensual sovereignty, as they cultivate present moment, body-centered awareness.

The more you practice this outside of your sexual experience, the easier it will be for you to access it during your sexual experience and vice-versa. It works both ways. The self-awareness and discoveries that you make during your sexual pleasure practice will also translate to your everyday life in truly rewarding and exceptional ways.

Reason #3 ~ Lack of sensation *(or sometimes even pain)* - Most women and *men* feel only a fraction of their full genital pleasure potential. Some of that is due to the reasons I have stated above; lack of education about their bodies, lack of present awareness in the body, but another key factor in genital sensitivity is emotion.

As I have stated throughout this book, the human body stores emotional imprints in the cellular tissue of the body, and any negative, painful, or uncomfortable sexual experience that we have had, as children or adults, can be stored in the genital tissue. The stored trauma or "stress" causes this area of the body to "numb-out" or shut down, and can moderately to severely impede a woman's ability to fully feel sexual sensation, sexual pleasure, and orgasm.

As I stated in Chapter 2, it is a commonly accepted fact that mental or emotional "stress" can cause a whole host of physical health issues such as headaches, ulcers, rashes, tight shoulder muscles, sore backs, etc. (I referred to this as the medical diagnosis of "pain disorder.")

We generally do not take into account the emotional/psychological effects of growing up in a culture which demonizes human sexual desire, (especially women's sexual desire), and yet plasters sexually suggestive images of men and women everywhere we look. These images encourage women (us) to dress provocatively, inciting sexual arousal, and yet we are not supposed to want sex for ourselves, and if we do, we should feel horribly guilty and ashamed (BAD GIRL).

Even if we have some level of sexual self-acceptance occurring, and we *don't* feel horribly guilty and ashamed of our sexuality, we have a whole culture of sexually repressed people (friends, families, associates, religious figures, MOVIES) repeatedly giving us the message that "**Good Girls** don't like sex, don't want sex, and don't openly discuss sex".

I recently saw this idea confirmed once again in the latest "Twilight" movie, where despite the massive sexual charge being portrayed between the female lead 'Bella' and the lead dude, 'Edward', Bella was to remain a "chaste" virgin until their impending marriage. Edward insisted on this, being "old-fashioned" as he was. And the father of the girl expressed tremendous approval for Edward's insistence that the couple adhere to these "old fashioned family values", despite the fact that both characters were 18 years old. Legal adults!

The recurring social sexual message that we get as women is "Good Girls are supposed to dress really sexy, act flirtatious and seductive, but pretend that they are completely sexually ignorant and deny the man for as long as possible." (This somehow makes us more desirable and arousing to them). Then when we do "give in", we moan and squeal for 2-7 minutes as if it's the best thing we ever experienced, and hope to God that this doesn't mean he'll take his love and affection away. We hope to God that he will call us the next day, even though we "gave him what he wanted" (not what we both wanted of course, because I'm a good girl!), and did the dirty deed of **having sex.** This creates a tremendous amount of mental and emotional confusion, which causes us to disconnect from our inner wisdom and guidance. This also generates sexually-related "stress" energy, some of which will be stored in the genital tissue.

The above is just one example explained in detail. There are a litany of other emotional/sexual traumas that can be stored in our genital tissue, causing us to lose connection with genital pleasure and sexual sensitivity.

Some sexual-emotional traumas or stresses are:

1) Religious guilt, fear, and shame
2) Being told as a child that touching your genitals is wrong, bad, or dirty
3) Being called a slut or "easy", for expressing your sensuality through clothing, dance, verbal discussions, or being sexually active
4) Being homosexual in a very heterosexually-oriented world
5) Being told that you smell bad (vaginal douche commercials)

6) Any sort of negative message about your sexual self-image such as "too fat", "too ugly", "too skinny", etc.
7) Messages about "family values" and natural sexual exploration being wrong
8) Your partner withdrawing emotionally after having sex
9) Wham, Bam, Thank-you Ma'am experiences
10) Your partner repeatedly ejaculating in 2-7 minutes, leaving you sexually frustrated
11) Emotionally disconnected sex
12) Violent sex, rape, sexual abuse
13) Any form of inappropriate touching at any age (i.e. being touched when you don't want to be touched).

When I began practicing Authentic Tantra® in 2008, I could have one clitoral orgasm, and I had no idea where my g-spot was, (or if it even existed). Sexual penetration was often painful and I thought that was just the way sex was supposed to be. I enjoyed sex, but found it somewhat uncomfortable, and had no real hope of actually having an orgasm during penetration. I thought sexual communication consisted of moaning really loudly for encouragement, or shifting my hips to get just the right angle of clitoral stimulation, hoping that my partner would interpret the meaning of my "body-language". I would never dream of self-stimulating in front of my lover, and vibrators were evil and scary devices.

I can now have anywhere from 5-30 orgasms in a lovemaking or self-pleasuring "session". I have clearly and distinctly experienced 10 of the 11 different orgasms that women can have, (multiple times in a row), and I consider communicating verbally to my partner about my pleasure, during pleasure, to be a *crucial* part of a mutually rewarding sexual experience. Adding to that, I can honestly say that some of the best sex I have ever had in my life has been with myself.

So how do we get from sensual imprisonment to sensual

sovereignty? How do we get from A to B? The magic is in the methods!

About The Methods ~ Vulva Massage and Self-Stimulation with Ocean Breath

I cannot over-emphasize the importance of using the ocean breath during your Vulva massage and self-pleasuring. Our natural reaction when we experience any sort of intense sensation or discomfort is to stop breathing and tighten up, or *contract*. Contraction is the opposite of being relaxed. It is a drawing up and pulling away of our awareness. We energetically *withdraw* from whatever area in which we are experiencing the discomfort or intensity. This internal recoil is the exact opposite of the energetic embodiment that we want to cultivate, yet it is currently our conditioned, habitual response to not just mild discomfort or pain, but also to intense pleasure as well.

One of the main habits that most women unconsciously perpetuate during sexual pleasure is to tighten the whole body and hold their breath, when they reach a certain point of sexual sensation. I believe this is due to the level of focused concentration typically needed to have a clitoral orgasm, especially with a partner. Placing all of that focus and concentration on that tiny little tip of pleasure, we hope and pray for that moment of climactic release, and that 1 tiny little orgasm that we get to have, if we are lucky.

Deep vaginal and full body orgasms are quite the opposite of the tight, coiled concentration I just described, and the ability to relax and open the body is absolutely essential for achieving transcendent states of pleasure. But before we get too far into orgasms, let's talk about preparing the body for pleasure with Vulva Massage.

Preparing the Body for Pleasure with Vulva Massage

You may remember me mentioning that it can take anywhere from 20-45 minutes for a woman's erectile tissue to fully engorge, and for her "sexual instrument" to be completely ready to be played. 20-45 minutes is a heck of a lot of conventional foreplay, hence the idea of "Preparing the Body for Pleasure" with Vulva Massage.

Vulva massage takes into account the physiology of our sexual response, and provides an easy, sensuous and pleasurable method for increasing the blood flow and circulation in the entire genital area. It also helps us get present with our genitals. Most of our genital touch is entirely for the purpose of 'washing or wetting', (cleaning or arousing) and rarely do we connect with our genitals as anything more than a functioning piece of the machinery.

Vulva massage works in much the same way as massaging any other area of the body.

When any area of the body is touched and manipulated with a certain degree of pressure, it stimulates blood flow and circulation in that area. It also helps clear out any toxins, lymph congestion, or stagnant emotional energy that may be stuck there. Some people consider whole body massage (not including the genitals) to be a fundamental aspect of maintaining good health and emotional balance.

Why wouldn't we want our vulvas and vaginas to experience the many wonderful, beneficial effects of sustained physical touch? When the ocean breath is added to this process, it helps us to a) relax and open our bodies so that any energy locked in that area will easily release, and b) feel more connected to the sensuality of the experience.

Instead of being in our heads *thinking* about how ridiculous we feel, or how uncomfortable it is to be massaging our vulvas, we use the breath as a tool to help us sense and *feel* into our bodies. This is what the term "embodying" really means to me: to fully inhabit every area of my body with present, relaxed awareness. The key to a truly rewarding sexual and life experience lies in our ability to relax and *feel*.

A little side note- I find it interesting that the main function that "Female Viagra" performs is to increase the blood flow and circulation in the genitals, thus enhancing a woman's ability to respond to sexual stimulation. Vulva massage has the same effect, and can be a natural alternative to female sexual dysfunctions that may be caused by lack of blood flow and circulation in the genital region.

Understanding Our Juicy Bits

After you have given yourself and (hopefully enjoyed) your Vulva Massage according to the instructions in your Self-Pleasuring Choreography at the end of this Chapter, you will be ready for some self-stimulation, a.k.a. Self-Pleasure!

If our goal is to cultivate our ultimate Pleasure Potential, (and indeed it is), then we need to know a bit more about our physiology, and the parts that we are working with.

Here I have outlined most of the highly erogenous zones of our sexual pleasure anatomy, as I understand them thus far. More and more is being discovered about female genital anatomy every day, and there are some amazing pioneers on the forefront of female sexual pleasure and orgasm. I encourage you to explore the reference materials that I have listed at the end of this book, in order to understand your body and pleasure with even greater depth.

The Clitoris - So much more than the tip of the iceberg that is visible, the clitoris is actually an entire system that consists of the head and shaft that we see, as well as legs, bulbs, and roots extending deep inside the body. According to recent studies, the head of the clitoris contains over 8,000 nerve endings, more than anywhere else in the entire body, and nearly twice as many as are in the head of the penis. [36] The clitoris is the only part of the human body designed solely for the purpose of providing pleasure.

The G-spot - A topic of much debate, the G-spot can be found in the first 1 – 1.5 inches inside the vagina, on the anterior wall (towards the front) of the body. If you took 1 finger right now, and put it inside your body, with the finger pointed up, you would feel a lump or ridge of rough, textured flesh that is distinctly different from the other smooth walls of the vagina. This is your G-spot and every woman has one. The reason many women don't experience, or know if they experience, g-spot orgasms can be found in the 3 reasons I listed in the beginning of this chapter which are: lack of education, lack of awareness, and MOSTLY, lack of sensation due to sexual-emotional trauma.

If you find your g-spot numb or painful during your loving self-stimulation, don't be alarmed. This is VERY common. I would say depending on the age group, at least 6 out of 10 women either a) don't know where their g-spot is, and/or b) have little to no sensation, or experience some form of pain or irritation when it is stimulated. But have no fear! Whatever your experience currently is, I can confidently say that it will change for the better over time, as you engage in The 4

---

[36] Robert Gonzales, JAN 16, 2012, http://io9.com/5876335/until-2009-the-human-clitoris-was-an-absolute-mystery

Principles of Self-Pleasure.

The A-spot - Otherwise known as the Anterior Fornix Erogenous Zone, the A-spot is located again on the anterior wall of the vagina, up past the g-spot, about 3-4 inches inside. You can find it by sitting in an upright, reclined position, and inserting your finger into your vagina, as far as it can comfortably go. The A-spot is conveniently located just about where the tip of your finger ends. I find that it is best stimulated with a sex toy, or someone else's fingers. It is simply a plexus of highly sensitive nerve endings, that when stroked repeatedly, can lead to deep, powerful, yummy orgasms. It is also said to be instrumental in vaginal lubrication.

The P Spot or Deep Spot - The Posterior Fornix Erogenous Zone is found deep inside the Vagina, in the area surrounding the cervix. This would technically be called the "The Deep Spot", though many people mistakenly refer to The A-spot as such. Regardless, the Posterior Fornix Erogenous zone is DEEP inside the Vagina and can best be reached by penetration with a sex toy or penis.

The Cervix - Recently Rutgers Psychology professor Dr. Komisaruk identified a "new" center of sexual sensation in women at the mouth of the cervix[37], though Tantrikas have known this for centuries. Yes the cervix is an erogenous zone, and can be highly pleasurable when gently massaged by your partner, or yourself.

In Tibetan Tantric instruction, the cervix is technically the

---

[37] Functional MRI of the Brain During Orgasm In Women, Barry R. Komisaruk   Beverly Whipple Rutgers, The State University of New Jersey, 2011

bottom end of the Central Channel, the core of the life force and *enlightened awareness* in the body. I personally have found cervical massage to be REALLY intense both physically and emotionally. I suggest proceeding with extreme caution in this particular area, especially if you have had any sexual abuse or physical trauma to the vagina or cervix itself.

The U-spot or Urethra - A network of spongy erectile tissue, which is called "the urethral sponge", surrounds the urethra. Many women find it very pleasurable to have the area around their urethral opening stimulated. The urethral sponge is part of the network of erectile tissue that makes up the g-spot.

The Perineal Sponge - This network of spongy erectile tissue is located between the anus and the vagina. It is an area of highly pleasurable sensation for many, but not all women.

The Anus - Some women find anal stimulation to be super arousing. A high concentration of pleasure-sensitive nerve endings can be found in and around the anus.

The Breasts and Nipples – This is another highly erogenous zone. Stimulation of our breast, particularly the nipples, promotes the production and release of oxytocin and prolactin.

In the same study by Dr. Komisaruk mentioned earlier regarding the cervix, magnetic resonance imaging showed that stimulating her nipples arouses the area of the sensory cortex in a woman's brain associated with the genitals.[38] In her book Emergence of the Sensual Woman, Saida Desilets states, "Massaging our nipples activates the endocrine system and

---

[38] Functional MRI of the Brain During Orgasm In Women, Barry R. Komisaruk   Beverly Whipple Rutgers, The State University of New Jersey, 2011

aids in the production of lubrication in our yoni."[39]

So once again we see that sexual stimulation not only feels good, but also it is actually good for us. *Like I've been saying....*

About Your Experience

I feel it's important to express that you are absolutely NOT required to enjoy every area that I described above. You may feel numb in some areas, pain in some areas, or simply do not want to go there right now. Whatever you are experiencing is okay and perfectly normal. However, please notice if there is an area that you have a particular aversion to, or find particularly uncomfortable or numb. Remember, I said that we store emotional imprints in the body, so chances are those areas of numbness, pain, or discomfort are areas of locked emotion. If the areas of numbness and pain are emotionally-based, they can and most likely will heal over time, with the application of the methods in this book. You will find your sexual pleasure awakening, your mind opening, and the way you experience your body changing.

(Note- there are some sexual dysfunctions that are physiologically based. In that case, please seek support from a medical professional.)

Another thing to keep in mind about your sexual awakening is the process of healing. Sensation returns in stages- the process usually going from numb, to pain, to irritation, to function or pleasure. Think of what happens when one of your limbs "falls asleep". First it goes numb, then it gets really painful as the blood rushes back in, then it gets tingly or irritated, then it's

---

[39] Emergence of The Sensual Woman, Saida Desilets, Jade Goddess Publishing, Wailea, Hawaii 2006

back to normal function. The process of healing in our sexual pleasure organs is exactly the same. You may go through all of those stages within a few minutes, few hours, few weeks, or a few months. It really depends on what has arisen to be healed and the depth of the trauma. I can say that using the Tantric meditations as outlined in Chapter 17 as part of your daily meditation *and* loving self-stimulation will significantly accelerate your process of sexual healing and sensual awakening.

The 11 (or more!) Different Flavors of Orgasm for Women

Most women have experienced a clitoral orgasm, though indeed some have not. Clitoral orgasms are what most women usually think of when they say the word "orgasm". This is simply because not many women know about, or are experiencing, their full potential for sexual pleasure, due to the many reasons that I have already stated. But our orgasmic potential is vast and seemingly infinite at times, and we have access to so much more than just that one type or 'flavor' of orgasm. I compare women's orgasmic potential vs. their current orgasmic experience to that of being at a buffet that serves 8-10 of their favorite foods, but only eating one dish for their entire lives, simply because nobody told them that there were 7-9 other dishes on the table waiting to be tasted and enjoyed.

In order to give you some clarity about your full sensual potential as a woman, and also some support and guidance around what you may have already experienced or soon will experience, I have outlined in this Chapter several of the different types or 'flavors' of orgasm that we as women are capable of experiencing.

Each area of our sexual pleasure is linked to a different neurological pathway in our bodies. This is why we can experience such a variety of flavors, textures and subtle notes in the symphony of female orgasm.[40]

The hypogastric nerve - transmits from the uterus and the cervix.

The pelvic nerve - transmits from the vagina and cervix.

The pudendal nerve - transmits from the clitoris.

The vagus nerve - transmits from the cervix, uterus and vagina

Apparently the vagus nerve also feeds the larynx as well, which is probably one the reasons that **unrepressed sound** is important to our orgasmic ability as women. This is why I encourage the use of the ocean breath during sexual stimulation in order to open the throat and subtle energetic channels of the body.

Sexual Biologist Art Noble shares that there are "14 different structures served by 4 nerve pathways in the female genitalia. 14! (14x13x12x....) is 84 billion. Considering that the vaginal nerve ending must be stimulated to get to the A spot and cervix, etc., that leaves about 50 billion different kinds of genital orgasms a woman can experience."[41]

Since very few of us are sexual biologists to the degree that we are aware which nerve ending is being stimulated at any given time, I have narrowed these 50 billion "flavors" of orgasm

---

[40] Shanna Freeman, 2012
http://science.howstuffworks.com/environmental/life/inside-the-mind/human-brain/brain-during-orgasm1.htm

[41] Art Noble, Author of The Sacred Female, Trafford Publishing (July 5, 2007)

down to the more digestible number of 11.

I have based the 11 types of orgasm on the area of the body in which we most directly perceive the orgasm, and the area in which we are usually experiencing the most direct sexual stimulation, at the time that the orgasmic experience occurs.

I am in no way suggesting that you *should* be having all 11 types of orgasm, or that you are inadequate in any way if that is not your current experience. Nor am I suggesting that you strive really hard to have any kind of orgasm, because that striving will separate you from your own pleasure.

I am simply sharing our potential as women. This is the full orgasmic capacity of the vehicle that we call a body. How very cool to know. When my true orgasmic ability began to emerge, I was amazed! I thought, how come nobody ever told me this was possible? I felt robbed of my sensual inheritance.

I share this with you so that you *know* what is possible, and can begin the process of reclaiming your birthright as a fully-integrated sensual-sexual human being.

You will notice that the 11 types of orgasm are also related to many of our highly erogenous zones. Go figure!

The 11 (or more!) types of Orgasm for Women are:

Clitoral

G-spot

U-spot

A-spot

Deep Spot or P-spot

Blended

Ejaculatory

Anal

Breast and Nipple

Uterine

Cervical

Whole Body (Bonus!)

1) *Clitoral Orgasms* are usually short and intense. They are often what we think of as a "climax". They can be most easily compared to a male ejaculatory orgasm.

2) *G-spot Orgasms* can vary from woman to woman, and session to session. At times they can be intense, but not quite as explosive as the clitoral orgasm, other times they can be experienced as very gentle, and almost imperceptible. It is generally a VERY different sensation than a clitoral orgasm. Often times it is better to stimulate the g-spot entirely on it's own, after you are already very aroused, in order to clearly discern the difference in sensation.

3) *U-Spot or Urethral Orgasms* arise from direct stimulation of the urethral opening.

4) *A-Spot Orgasms* are a deeper vaginal orgasm than the G-spot, and are best reached with the fingers of a partner, or specific sex toy.

5) *P-Spot Orgasms* can be very powerful and usually occur with very deep, prolonged vaginal penetration with either a penis or a dildo.

6) *Blended Orgasms* usually include the clitoris and can be a combination any of those other spots at the same time, though most people initially experience them as a g-spot - clitoral orgasm. I myself have experienced

    clitoral- anal- g-spot orgasm,

    clitoral- a-spot orgasm,

    clitoral- cervical- g-spot orgasm,

    you get the picture.

7) *Ejaculatory Orgasms* for most women tend to be a result of direct G-spot or A-spot stimulation, though women are capable of ejaculating without orgasm. My partners' fingers and The Honey Dipper Wand are the best tools that I have encountered thus far for stimulating this type of orgasm. The actual methods for achieving this type of orgasm are best learned in person, with a visual aid of some sort. (I usually demonstrate the techniques on a rubber model)

8) *Anal Orgasms* can be very fulfilling for many women. Some women love anal intercourse, for others it's a "no deal." If it is new territory for you, I suggest starting small and slow. There are a number of sex toys available for anal pleasure. In choosing one, just remember non-porous and body safe!

9) *Nipple or Breast Orgasms* are apparently stimulated from the intracostal nerve pathway and triggered by the production of oxytocin, which causes pleasurable uterine contractions.[42] Some women have experienced orgasm while breast-feeding, which makes sense as oxytocin is

---

[42] Art Noble, Author of The Sacred Female, Trafford Publishing (July 5, 2007

produced in huge quantities during that life-giving activity.

10) *Uterine Orgasms* can be felt deep in the belly and are usually a result of deep and prolonged sexual penetration.

11) *Cervical Orgasms* can be experienced from direct stimulation to the cervix with fingers, sex toys or a penis.

And One More Special Bonus Orgasm!

12) *Whole Body Orgasms* are like electric ripples from the top of your head to the tips of your toes. Whole body orgasms can be a result of supercharged sexual energy flowing through all of your subtle channels and meridians. For me, these types of orgasm happened after several hours of sexual stimulation with a partner, but others have reported having them through deep breathing practices alone.

What's so great about orgasm?

Other than the feelings of bliss, joy, euphoria, and the many physiological health benefits of orgasm, some people may wonder "what's the big deal about orgasm?" especially if their experiences haven't been particularly rewarding up to this point. You may remember me mentioning in the beginning of this book the Secret Tibetan Teaching that every orgasm is a glimpse or taste of Enlightenment. Science has shown without a doubt that orgasm is a mind-altering experience, which has highly beneficial effects upon our emotional, mental, and physical health.

According to research done by New Brain - New World, during the experience of orgasm "There will be an increase of slow brain waves such as delta and theta waves. The stronger the waves, the more orgasmic energy you can hold in your consciousness."[43]

What's so great about that? Apparently, according to energy healer and scientist Brent Philips "while in the Theta state, the mind is capable of deep and profound learning, healing, and growth - it is the brain wave where our minds can connect to the Divine and manifest changes in the material world." He goes on to say "Theta is the border between the conscious and the subconscious world, and by learning to use a conscious, waking Theta brain wave we can access and influence the powerful subconscious part of ourselves that is normally inaccessible to our waking minds."[44]

Additionally Delta brainwaves provide us with increased empathy, and access to the "unconscious mind". Being in delta is like being in the most deeply relaxing trance or non-physical awareness. Delta brainwave patterns have also been linked to speed healing of the mind and body.

4 Mind 4 Health.com, a website devoted to mental health and research states that "Researchers have discovered that within the delta brainwave range, some frequencies are even able to produce healthy substances such as: DHEA, melatonin, and H.G.H. (Human Growth Hormone). The melatonin, H.G.H. (human growth hormone), and DHEA that delta brain waves produce are able to slow and or reverse the effects of aging."

Delta brainwaves have been shown to reduce production of the stress hormone cortisol, the presence of which has been

---

43

http://www.newbrainnewworld.com/?Awakening_of_Kundali
ni:Kundalini_and_Sex
[44] http://www.formulaformiracles.net/brain-waves.html

proven to accelerate the aging process in mammals.[45]

Human Sexual Orgasm gives us direct access to these brainwave patterns, which have been shown to have profoundly healing and regenerative effects on our mind and body. These brainwave patterns also give us direct access to deeper levels of self-awareness, self-connection, and "enlightened" states of mind. **That's** what's so great about orgasm!

"Forget about the fast lane. If you really want to fly, just harness your power to your passion".

~ Oprah ~

---

[45] http://4mind4life.com/

The Practice of The Art of Self-Pleasure ~

In this section I have outlined the choreography for your dance of self-love. I encourage you to read it through step by step a few times, before getting down to business. Also, do feel free to keep the guide handy during your first few practice runs. Some of my students keep their guidebooks right next to them for easy reference of the techniques during their self-pleasuring practice.

I am giving you suggestions for a very basic self-pleasuring session below. Again, please feel free to embellish them as you desire. I often begin my self-pleasuring sessions with a hot fragrant bath, warm coconut oil all over my body, and some sensual dance for myself in the mirror. I encourage you to be creative and discover ways to enrich the sensuality of your sexual experiences.

Be sure to create an inviting space that nourishes your 5 senses for your self-pleasure practice. Stimulate visual pleasure with a tidy area and candles, flowers, etc. Stimulate smell with incense, or aromatherapy oils. Stimulate sound with music, taste with flavored water, wine, or yummy fruits, and use an organic body oil or sensual lubricant to enhance touch. Be sure to have your recommended sex toys laid out right next to you for easy access. Also be sure to have plenty of hand towels nearby to wipe off occasionally slippery hands.

The physical posture for self-pleasuring is very important. When we masturbate, we tend to lie flat on our backs, with our eyes closed, which I believe prevents us from remaining fully present with our experience. I suggest that you are in a somewhat upright and reclined position, as if you are reclined and reading in bed. This gives you access to your entire vulva and vagina, and makes it easier for you to use the recommended sex toys (think leverage), as well as remaining present with your emotional-sexual experience. *(See fig. 1)*

1) Begin with meditation to cultivate present, relaxed awareness with focus.

Sitting in an upright position with the spine straight, begin following 21 breaths, proceed to color breathing, and fire element meditation.

2) When you are done meditating, relax back into a comfortable reclined position and placing one hand over your heart center, and one hand over genitals, and practice your Ocean Breath to connect deeply to your sensual self-awareness. *(See fig. 1)* Continue this until you feel "full".

3) Continue your Ocean Breath with an open mouth and gentle sounds, lovingly caress and stroke your body from the top down to help balance the wind energies of your body. Continue this self-stroking until you naturally want to begin your Vulva massage. Be intuitive, organic, and follow what feels good.

4) Begin your Vulva massage as outlined in the diagram entitled "Vulva Massage" at the end of this Chapter. Please remember to use your ocean breath during the whole process and take your time! Enjoy your massage with an attitude of innocence, grace, and curiosity.

5) Add non-toxic, organic lube, and begin pleasuring your clitoris with your *fingers first*. I believe it is important for us to

make a tactile connection to our bodies initially, in order to create a kinesthetic awareness of our sexual pleasure organs. As you feel your clitoris begin to swell, take the well-lubed ring finger of your left hand, and gently insert it into your vagina, palm up, while using the ocean breath.

6) Feel the textured ridge of tissue located towards the front of your body. This is your G-spot! Notice the size, texture, and any sensations of pleasure or pain. Generally your g-spot is not going to be incredibly responsive this early in the game. As you become more sexually aroused, the g-spot will engorge and become very full and erect. This is generally when women will experience the most sensation and pleasure in this area.

7) Remove your finger from the g-spot, (the initial contact is just to say "hello"), and begin pleasuring your clitoris with a recommended vibrator, or continue with your fingers.

Generally our habit is to pleasure just our clitoris until we reach climax. That is great, but will not give you access to the other types of orgasm. So for this purpose, we will use the clitoris as our "arousal button", getting our bodies warmed up and full of pleasure juices, and then we will "back off" the button for a bit, in order to explore these other pleasure zones.

8) When your clitoral pleasure has reached about a 6 or 7 on a scale of 1-10, begin using the honey dipper wand on your g-spot. Be sure it is well lubed for penetration.

Now the dance begins! For the next part you will be using both the honey dipper on your g-spot, and the vibrator (or fingers) on your clitoris, at the same time and alternating.

Your next steps will be determined by which of the following experiences most applies to you. A) You will either feel pleasure when you stimulate your g-spot or B) you will experience something other than pleasure, which may include very little to no sensation (numb) irritation, or pain.

A) **If you have lots of pleasure in your g-spot -** just go for it! The key to multiple orgasms is learning to really relax with your pleasure, instead of contract around it. Relaxing and opening the body with the ocean breath allows the pleasure to build and for the energy to "rise higher" so that the orgasm is a more full-bodied experience, and less genitally-oriented. It allows for a "higher grade" or quality of orgasm. Use your ocean breath with SOUND the entire time, and most especially when you are at a 9 on your scale. *Relax* into the pleasure, relax, relax, relax and ride the waves of bliss.

B) **If you have little to no sensation in your g-spot -** stimulate the clitoris and g-spot at the same time until you reach about an 8.5 or 9 on a pleasure scale of 1-10. Then stop clitoral stimulation and focus on just the g-spot. Remember the g-spot responds to more and more pressure as it becomes more and more engorged, hence the need for leverage. Continue stimulating the g-spot for a little while without any clitoral stimulation, and just notice whatever sensations you are experiencing. If you continue to feel numbness, or any discomfort, continue re-introducing clitoral stimulation. "Dance" back and forth until you begin feeling pleasure in your g-spot, or have an orgasm. Just as I stated above, use the ocean breath to relax and open the body, and be sure to make *sound*.

*It is **very** important for us to express our sexual pleasure through sound. It allows for the free flow of energy throughout our entire body.*

The key to releasing sexual emotional trauma is to pleasure yourself, and allow that pleasure to unlock the trauma stored in the cellular tissue of the body. Then simply relax by using the ocean breath, and allow the body to do what it was designed to do. Allow whatever experiences arise to occur without pulling away or shutting down. You may feel a variety of emotions or physical sensations such as irritation, annoyance, pain, sadness, confusion, or just be plain uncomfortable. Whatever you are experiencing is perfectly normal, perfectly okay, and *will change!* It is all part of the process of sexual healing and sensual awakening.

The body is designed to heal itself and all we need to do is provide the support necessary for it to do its job. The Restorative Yoga philosophy is "support stimulates release". In this case the support that you are bringing is pleasure, breath, and your relaxed awareness.

To awaken your other "pleasure zones" you simply need different tools, though the process is the same. Please note that when working the g-spot and deeper vaginal zones, it is important to remove clitoral stimulation at times, in order to feel more deeply into the vagina. The clitoris can keep our awareness more superficially focused. When you feel pleasure deep in the vagina, remove clitoral stimulation, and just feel the vaginal sensations for a while. Then play with bringing clitoral stimulation back in, to enhance the experience.

We tend to have an over-dependence on the clitoris, but once the cells of the vagina remember their pleasure potential, we need less and less clitoral stimulation after a certain point. I like to say that the clitoris is like the little engine that drives the pleasure. Once we get to a certain point of vaginal pleasure in our session, the clitoris is awesome as an enhancer, but not necessarily as the main place of focus.

In the beginning I suggest doing your self-pleasuring sessions about once a week, or more if you can. Again though, this is about cultivating pleasure, so if it begins to feel like a chore, and not a joy, check in with yourself about what would meet your needs for sensual pleasure more effectively. Maybe you just want a good old-fashioned masturbation session instead of a doing your self-pleasuring "homework." Go for it! Remember this is about you becoming deeply attuned and aware of your own individual needs for pleasure. There is magic in those moments that we connect with what our needs are, and what actions would most effectively meet those needs.

Soul empowerment comes from having the internal freedom to know, understand, and take action to meet our own needs for passion, pleasure, joy, and self-expression

"Woman must not accept; she must challenge. She must not be awed by that which has been built up around her; she must reference that woman in her which struggles for expression."

~ Margaret Sanger ~

The Art of Self- Pleasure For Women
Instructional Diagrams

Fig. 1- Begin your vulva massage in an upright, relaxed position. Be sure to have lots of pillows behind your back for comfort and support. Make a heart to genital connection, and then begin your meditation.

Fig. 2- After completing your meditation, relax your back against the pillows, and proceed with the Ocean Breath. Be sure to start with one hand over your heart center and one hand over your vulva. Sensuously stroke your body, while continuing the Ocean Breath

The Art Of Self-Pleasure Vulva Massage

1. Begin by placing one hand over your heart and one hand over your Vulva while doing "The Ocean Breath"
2. Grasp the fleshy area of your Mons Pubis and massage firmly with your fingertips. (A)
3. Continue the massage down your outer labia, massaging each one individually. (B)
4. Massage the outer labia all the way to the bottom, ending near your anus (C)
5. Use your fingertips to massage into your pelvic floor. Find the ridge of bone that defines your pelvic cavity, and gently massage up past the bones, into your pelvic floor area. (D)
6. Next, take your entire vulva in both hands and apply pressure while you squeeze the labia together as firmly as you comfortably can, making a "vulva taco" (E)
7. Then use your fingertips to grasp and massage your inner labia, from top to bottom. (F)
8. Massage the clitoral shaft individually by grasping it gently between your thumb and forefinger, and make a gentle rolling motion. (G)
9. Lastly, apply a generous amount of lubricant to the palms of both hands, and stroke the entire vulva from bottom to top, alternating hands as you go. Make sure the palm of your hand cover your entire vulva, applying light pressure as you stroke.
10. When you are ready, begin pleasuring yourself as described in Chapter 19.

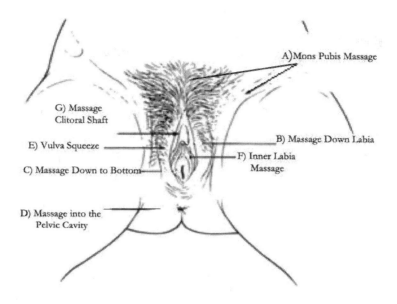

A) Mons Pubis Massage

G) Massage Clitoral Shaft

E) Vulva Squeeze

C) Massage Down to Bottom

D) Massage into the Pelvic Cavity

B) Massage Down Labia

F) Inner Labia Massage

Please experiment with different degrees of pressure and various strokes. Please explore, invent and discover what you enjoy. Notice the difference in the way your body responds to sexual stimulation, when you begin by preparing your body for pleasure with vulva massage.

"If we don't change, we don't grow. If we don't grow, we are not really living. Growth demands a temporary surrender of security."

~ Gail Sheehy ~

Chapter 20. Sex Toys For Tantra ~ What to use and how to choose!

Every Art has its respective "tools of the trade." Painters have paintbrushes, sculptors have knives, and master carpenters have entire tool- boxes of assorted instruments to help them get the job done with efficiency and ease. In the case of The Art of Self-Pleasure, there are some recommended "tools" for facilitating the awakening of your full orgasmic pleasure potential.

When I initially began my sexual awakening journey, I was completely ignorant about sex toys. At that time I was a firm believer of a "fingers only" approach, and as I have previously stated, I was horrified at, (and terrified of), the idea of actually putting something other than a man's penis inside my vagina.

Because an integral part of my Authentic Tantra® training included long-periods of self-stimulation, with a focus on the g-spot and other internal erogenous zones, I quickly realized that I was going to need the support of tools made specifically for the purpose of enhancing sexual pleasure.

Because of my complete ignorance regarding sex toys, I initially wasted a lot of money and time on products that were supposed to be "the best g-spot toy ever", or had reached mass appeal like the many versions of "The Rabbit". I generally bought the least expensive toy I could find with absolutely no regard for the material it was made of, or the efficiency of the design. I didn't know the difference between battery-operated toys vs. rechargeable, Silicone vs. Jelly, hard plastic vs. velvetcote.

The good news is- after all of that failure and frustration, I can now provide you with what I consider to be some of the most pertinent information regarding sexual pleasure enhancing products.

What's it made of?

The material that your sex toy is made out of is of vital importance. Don't be fooled into buying inexpensive toys made with harmful toxic materials. Many low-quality sex toys are made out of plastic that contains phthalates and other harmful materials. Below is a list of what to watch out for, and in which products these potentially harmful and toxic materials are generally found. There are a variety of women-owned, health-conscious, online sex toy stores. My Two favorite sex toy awareness resources are Babeland Toys and Holistic Wisdom.com. They are both absolutely stellar resources for education regarding the safety of almost every sex toy material available today. Babeland Toys is based out of Seattle, Washington, and has been a leader in creating sex-positive education and experiences for women all over North America. Most of the information below is compiled from these two resources.

Phthalates - are used to soften vinyl and are often found in jelly style sex toys. They are thought to leach out of the plastic and into your bloodstream. Phthalates act as an endocrine disruptor and are linked to diabetes, breast cancer, reduced sperm count, ADHD, liver damage, insulin resistance, metabolic interference (contributing to obesity), asthma and allergies, premature breast development in girls, abnormal genital development in males (small penis, un-descended testicles), autism and low birth weight in infants.[46]

Parabens – are found in most commercially available

---

[46] http://www.holisticwisdom.com/toxic-sex-toys.htm

lubricants. Parabens are known to alter estrogen in women, increasing related diseases such as breast tumors, heighten allergic reactions, and accelerate the development of skin cancer, as well as decrease sperm cell count in men.

Triclosan – is found in sex toy cleaners and genital "cleansing" products. Triclosan is an endocrine disrupter that has been linked to allergies, creating bacterial resistance, and abnormal thyroid functioning.

2-Butoxyethanol - is found in sexual products such as dildos and vibrators with latex paints, sex toy cleaners in the form of liquid soaps, and cosmetics. It causes irritation of mucous membranes of the throat, nose and eyes.

About Quality

With sex toys, you really do get what you pay for. Consider your sex toy an investment in your sexual health and spiritual growth. Save up and get a good one, or 2, or 3. Don't fall for the $20 sex toy special. Those toys are usually NOT body-safe and chances are they WILL break in a relatively short period of time, and with very few uses.

About Design

Even though there is an overwhelming variety of sex toys, there are really only a few basic designs or "styles," repeated over and over again, with slight variations on the theme. I have included most of the styles that I like best for the specific purpose of awakening our full orgasmic pleasure potential. And there is always more to learn! I encourage you to visit my website feminine-emergence.com for ongoing updates to my list of preferred sexual enhancement products.

My recommendations

All of the toys/tools that I have included in this book are made of high-quality, body-safe materials. I have tried almost every body safe material on the market, and hands down, my personal favorite sex toy material (with the exception of the honey dipper wand) is 100% medical grade silicone. There are a few reasons for silicone being my favorite pleasure product material. 1) The texture is usually very soft (almost velvety against your sexual pleasure parts), and 2) it is non-porous, meaning it won't hold bacteria that can cause infection later. It also carries vibration like nothing else, so you get more buzz for your buck, so to speak. 100% medical grade silicone sex toys tend to be pricey, and they are absolutely worth every penny that you spend. So make the investment. They are usually rechargeable, which means they make less noise than battery operated toys, and usually come with some kind of warranty.

So, without further ado, let me introduce my top **sex toys for tantra** suggestions. You will find them all available for sale on my website under products.

For The G-Spot

#1) The crystal honey dipper wand...deluxe. The angle on this toy makes it *superb* for direct **g-spot stimulation.** There is just nothing else like it for **your g-spot.** 100% Lucite, which makes it light-weight (easy on the wrist), non-porous, body-safe, easy to sterilize. The absolute best toy on the market for opening and activating **the g-spot in women AND men. Also a great toy for A-Spot stimulation.**

#2) The Gi-ki by Je Joue - Smooth yet firm, with a wide soft head makes this toy awesome for direct g-spot stimulation. I like to use this one a little later in the session, when my g-spot is already nice and engorged, and I want more depth and

fullness than the crystal wand can provide. If your g-spot is already pretty juicy, I recommend this toy to keep it going, and take it to the next level!

For The A-spot and deep penetration

#3) The Elise by Lelo - Just past **the g-spot**, is a little piece of heaven called **'The A-spot'**. Usually somewhat difficult to reach by yourself, the Elise makes that sweet bliss easier to access. It also hits all those juicy deep areas at the **back of the vagina**, that rarely get as much love and attention as they need. Another 100% medical grade silicone, non-porous, body-safe toy.

#4) The Mona by Lelo- Same idea as the Elise, with less depth and more of an angle, makes it great **for g-spot play** as well as **A-spot.**

For Clitoral Stimulation

#5) The Siri by Lelo- The Siri is small, compact, and fits in the palm of your hand, which is why I like it! The Siri has a medical grade silicone tip, and a multitude of vibrations ranging from powerful to subtle, at the tip of your fingers.

#6) The WeVibe Touch Made out of 100% medical grade silicone, this entire vibrator hummmms...! Waterproof and powerful, this is better than your finger, in so many ways. Awesome for solo and partner play.

I have also included a body-safe, non-toxic lube recipe that you can make at home, that also serves the purpose of a great skin conditioner and massage oil (go figure!) Other natural commercially-available lube suggestions can be found on my website as well.

Authentic Tanta Master and Tibetan Holistic Healer, Jacques Drouin created this natural lubricant for his student and clients. Jacques is the Founder of Tantric Arts of Love and Co-Founder of Authentic Tantra®

In an 8-12 ounce bottle mix:

- 3 parts organic coconut oil
- 1-2 parts organic Aloe Vera Gel or fresh washed and peeled Aloe
- 1-2 Parts Organic Olive Oil
- 5-10 drops of essential Lavender and/or Ylang-Ylang oil

By Adding 5 – 10 drops of essential Lavender oil, and/or Ylang-Ylang oil to your organic, non-toxic lube, you can naturally create the experience of commercially available, and usually toxic "warming lubes". Both oils bring a warming and tingling sensation to the genitals, naturally increasing blood flow, circulation, and thus sensation in that area.

Note- every body enjoys a slightly different degree of viscosity. Please adjust the recipe to your requirements. When using a condom, use less olive oil, and more aloe vera gel, to prevent breakage.

"It is good to have an end to journey towards,

but it is the journey that matters, in the end."

~ Ursula K Le Guin ~

Chapter 21. The Secret Jade Ben Wa Ball "Sexercises"

I teach The Secret Jade Ben Wa Ball "Sexercises" in my Feminine Emergence Dance Classes and Sensual Awakening for Women Workshops, for the purpose of supporting women in cultivating a lifetime of genital health and sexual enjoyment.

When I began my study and practice of Authentic Tantra®, I was surprised at the significant role that vaginal and pelvic floor strength played, not just in our sexual health and pleasure, but also in the health and wellness of our entire bodies.

According to ancient Taoist sexual practices, women with undeveloped vaginal tonicity may tend to "leak chi" through the vaginal opening, especially during menstruation. This may result in a continued loss of vital energy, and feelings of chronic exhaustion or depletion.[47]

They also state that vaginal "tonicity" is a key factor in aging and weight control, as the temperature of the sexual organs is an important factor in regulating the metabolism of fats. A cold genital zone indicates a slower metabolism.

Because these exercises increase circulation throughout the sexual organs, they increase the warmth and health of the sexual reproductive system, preventing many illnesses that

---

[47] http://www.healingtao.org/deutsch/beschreib22.htm

may result from a stagnation of energy in the genitals. [48]

Some illnesses that can occur as a result of stagnation in the genital zone are: chronic vaginal and urinary tract infections, endometriosis, fibroids, vaginal discharge, menstrual problems, bloating, cramps, irregular periods, and a whole host of other female "complaints".[49]

The Pelvic Floor

The pelvic floor rests like a hammock at the base of the pelvic girdle. These muscles support the bladder, uterus and rectum, and basically hold-up our internal organs.

The pelvic floor muscles also regulate the **downward voiding winds**, which are energy currents in the body that are responsible for retaining and excreting urine, feces, semen, menstrual blood, female ejaculate and orgasm.[50]

When these muscles are healthy and strong, we naturally retain our vital chi, and the downward voiding activity of the body functions with greater efficiency and ease.

Strong vaginal and pelvic floor muscles are essential for enhanced sexual pleasure, as these are the muscles that rhythmically contract during orgasm i.e.; the stronger they are, the deeper and more powerful the orgasm. Strong and healthy pelvic floor muscles also contribute to clitoral sensitivity, and support the healthy engorgement of the erectile tissue located

---

[48] Uta Demontis http://www.manawa.co.uk/
[49] http://www.acupuncture-online.com/focus.htm
[50] Jacques Drouin, Tibetan Holistic Healing
http://tibetanholistichealing.com/

in and around the vagina.

(In men, pelvic floor exercises have been found to increase the strength, frequency, and duration of their erections, and can assist men in achieving a greater degree of ejaculation control.)

You can easily identify your Pelvic Floor muscles by stopping the flow of urine several times midstream. (This is also an excellent way of getting some "sexercises" in during the day!)

Most people are familiar with the term "Kegel exercise", and generally associate them with women recovering vaginal "tone" after childbirth. Traditionally known as Vaginal Kung-fu, **Jade Egg and Ben Wa Ball** exercises are similar to Kegels, *but better.*

Jade Ben Wa Balls greatly enhance the efficacy of Kegel type exercises by giving the body an object to "grip" and tense around. The movement of the Jade balls inside the vagina also has the effect of stimulating reflexology points located inside the vaginal canal, thus contributing to the over-all health of all the major organs.

The energetic quality of Jade helps to balance the yin energies of a woman's body and acts as medicine for the vaginal tissue, having the ability to absorb, heal and transform "negative" energy that may be held there.

Doing Jade Ben Wa Ball exercises is especially recommend for women who have given birth, (obviously), but they are also highly recommended before giving birth, as strong and healthy pelvic floor muscles may contribute to an easier labor and birthing process. Also, doing these exercises creates more awareness of our vaginas, a really important factor in having an easeful birthing process!

Many women have found that doing these exercises has helped relieve vaginal pain and dryness, and many menopausal women have found that doing Jade Ball exercises has helped them to re-lubricate naturally. In fact in Taoist sexuality, these exercises are prescribed to women specifically for this purpose.

Below are the Jade Ben Wa Ball exercises that I teach in my classes, workshops, and private coaching sessions. Another great way to use these exercises is with the Feminine Emergence DVD, which I designed intentionally to be used in conjunction with the Jade Ben Wa Balls.

I strongly recommend purchasing your Jade Egg or Ben Wa Balls pre-drilled. This helps with the easy removal of the balls after use, and prevents them from getting "accidentally" stuck inside you. (This has happened to me on more than one occasion, so I am quite adamant about using drilled and properly threaded balls!)

To begin you will want to thread your Jade Ben Wa Balls with un-waxed, unflavored Dental floss. Use about 6 inches of string, thread through hole and tie off end 4x. (Please remember to thread each ball individually!)

Then you will squat down and insert Ben Wa Balls one at a time, kind of like a tampon. (Please feel free to use lube if you like.)

Stand-up and give them a big squeeze, and you are now ready for your exercises!

Jade Ben Wa Ball "Sexercises" as taught by Devi Ward at Feminine Emergence

1) Stand up with your feet shoulder width apart, knees slightly bent, pelvis in a neutral position. Visualize a red sphere of light in your pelvis.

2) Curl your pelvis forward at the same time as you contract your entire pelvic floor as tightly as you can. This will include your rectum, your vagina, and your buttocks. Inhale and curl the pelvis forward while contracting the vaginal and pc muscles. At the top of your inhalation, hold the contracting for 3-5 seconds, then exhale as you release back to starting position. Relax the entire pelvic floor at the end of your exhalation for 3 seconds before beginning your contraction again. The relaxation is just as important as the contraction, as it prevents creating a chronically tight muscle, which is unhealthy.

- **Repeat 5 - 10 standing "pelvic curls" with deep vaginal contraction.**

3) Repeat these same exercises, but exhale on the contraction, and inhale on the release. This works both the downward voiding and ascending wind energies of the body.

- **Repeat 5 - 10 standing "pelvic curls" exhaling on the contraction**

4) Next, allowing the pelvis to remain in neutral position, focus on just the vaginal muscles. Visualize the Ben Wa Balls as red spheres of light. In Taoist sexual practices, the vagina is said to have 3 chambers, bottom, middle and top, each with subtly distinct muscle fibers, which can be developed to create vaginal dexterity.

   - Begin by starting at the bottom/vaginal opening.
   - As you inhale, contract bottom, middle, and top, imagining the red spheres of light moving up the vagina, towards the cervix.
   - At the top of the inhalation, deepen contraction as tightly as you can, then exhale as you release slowly back down, top, middle, bottom (vaginal opening). Relax your muscles completely at the bottom of exhalation.
   - **Repeat 5 - 10 x's.**

5) Next, lie down flat on your back, with your knees up, and feet flat on the floor. Tug on the strings lightly to sense ball placement inside the vagina. (I like to see how far they've moved)
   - Continuing to visualize red light, while contracting the 3 chambers of the vagina with inhalation, and release back down with exhalation. (This is the same exercise that you just did standing, but now you are lying down. This helps you to tune into the subtle fluctuations with a bit more acuity.
   - **Repeat 5 - 10 x's.**

6) Remaining on the floor, do 5 or more of the pelvic curls that you previously did standing up. (The first exercise, but lying down on your back).
   - Being sure to keep your tailbone on the floor as you curl upwards, bear down on the

exhalation/release, like you are pushing out urine really forcefully. (This helps to develop the downward voiding activity, which is essential for ejaculation.)
- **Repeat this 5-10x's**

7) Lastly inhale and hold while rapidly squeezing and releasing the superficial muscles of your vulva and vagina. Almost like making your clitoris pulse.
   - Do 5-10 "pulses" or rapid contract and release.
   - Exhale and hold your exhalation while doing 5-10 pulses
   - **Repeat this process 2-4 times**

When finished remove the balls, and wash immediately. Be sure to remove strings and replace them with each use. I suggest boiling the balls to disinfect them once a week or more and soak them in salt water often to "clear" the energy. To prevent irritation, wash your Ben Wa Balls with whatever soap you use in and on your vulva and vagina.

"Courage is like a muscle. We strengthen it with use."

~ Ruth Gordon ~

Chapter 22. The Shake Your Soul-Song Pleasure Program

The 'Shake Your Soul-Song Pleasure Program' uses all 4 of The Principles of Self-Pleasure as a foundation for creating better physical, mental and emotional health, and sensual-sexual joy. The minimum format for your Pleasure Program will be 20-30 minutes in the morning, 5-10 minutes in evening, 3-4 times a week, and 1 sensual self-pleasuring sessions once every 10 days or more.

The program guide is designed for you to easily "weave" these teachings into your everyday life, so that they become an enhancement, rather than a chore or just another "thing to do". You can follow the program guide exactly or change things around as needed to suit your life and schedule.

Your Pleasure Program guide is as follows ~

1) Begin the day by cultivating Self-Pleasure Principles #1 and #2. The Movement will get your chi (energy) moving for the day, and the Meditation will help establish a more peaceful and balanced state of mind.

Self-Pleasure Principle #1 ~ Movement ~ I recommend that you begin with putting in your Jade Ben Wa Balls if you have them, and using them in conjunction with the Feminine Emergence DVD ~ "Celebration."

Practice The 5 Core Pelvic Movements with the Jade Ben Wa Ball "Sexercises" for 20 minutes.

Self-Pleasure Principle #2 ~ Meditation ~ When you are done with your movement, sit quietly and follow your Authentic

Tantra® Meditation as outlined in Chapter 17. This generally will take about 10-15 minutes.

Then enjoy your day! Pay attention and notice any changes in your energy levels throughout the day. Over the coming weeks observe any changes in your thought patterns and emotional disposition towards life.

2) I personally enjoy ending my day with Pleasure Principle #3, as I find it easier to take some quiet time for self-reflection later in the evening, when all the busy-ness of the day is done. That being said, I encourage you to "weave" this exercise in wherever and whenever it fits best.

Self-Pleasure Principle #3 ~ Self-Connection ~ Begin by lying on your back and doing the Ocean Breath for about 2-5 minutes. No need to time this exactly, just go by your intuition. When you are done, sit upright and begin your Pleasure Journal as outlined in Chapter 18.

3) It's important that you practice Pleasure Principle #4 with a degree of consistency, but without it feeling like a chore. Depending on your lifestyle it can be very difficult to take time out of your busy schedule to pleasure yourself sexually, especially for longer than the few minutes it usually takes to have a clitoral orgasm. I encourage you to start where you are and start small if necessary. There is no need to feel overwhelmed with the thought of scheduling hours and hours out of your life to cultivate your sexuality. Even if you are able to spend 20 minutes once every 10 days touching yourself and exploring your sensual-sexual pleasure you will be transforming your life and your relationship to your body in measurable lasting ways.

Self-Pleasure Principle #4 ~ Self-Stimulation or The Art of Self-Pleasure ~ I encourage women to make sensual pleasure dates with themselves. Decide a day and/or a few days and times that will work for you to explore your sexual pleasure for a minimum of 20 minutes. And then, *put it on your calendar, enter it into your phone, whatever you have to do to "carve it in stone"*. **This is a date with you**. Prioritize it, just like you would a date with a really hot and sexy prospective or current partner. Then follow the Self-Pleasure Choreography outlined for you in Chapter 19.

There are a few products that I recommend for your Pleasure Program. All of these items with the exception of the Pleasure Journal can be found at Feminine - Emergence.com.

1. The Feminine Emergence DVD~ Celebration which includes instruction in The 5 Core Pelvic Movements

2. Jade Ben Wa Balls or Jade Egg

3. The Crystal Honey Dipper G-spot Wand

4. Pleasure Journal

Using all of these "tools" together has the potential to create an entirely new experience of sexual-sensual pleasure and thus our very lives.

"When we change ourselves, we change the world"

~ Author Unknown~

Recent Testimonial of The Shake Your Soul-Song Pleasure Program ~

"I have been practicing The 4 Forms of Pleasure: dancing, meditating, journaling and self pleasuring for a few months and already it is transforming my life.

Prior to my experience, I was very uncomfortable with my body and sexuality. Through sacred erotic dance I have learned to connect with my feminine essence and to cultivate self-love and acceptance. When watching myself dance in the mirror I have noticed that my inner voice actually finds the way my body moves quite sexy:)

I now wake up excited to begin my days with the 5 core pelvic movements along with the fire meditation as these have helped me release emotional pain and severe tightness in my hips.

Also, I am extremely grateful for the opportunity to have learned the art of self -pleasure. Until recently, I didn't know where my g spot was and upon discovery noticed that it had little sensation.

Now I have a regular self-pleasuring routine and from this my g spot has gone from numb to painful, to recently experiencing pleasure.

My vulva massages have taught me to be a kind and gentle lover with myself and have allowed me to reawaken a part of my body that has been dormant most of my life.

It is very self-empowering to realize that I am my greatest lover and to have sexual experiences that I didn't even know were possible.

I want to thank you for opening my eyes and my heart to a deeper level of self-connection and love." ~ J.J. Vancouver, B.C.

"Life is either a daring adventure or nothing."

~ Helen Keller ~

Resources and More to Learn

Here I have listed resources for further learning. I have referenced many of these books and their authors throughout Shake Your Soul Song. All of the resources that I have listed here have in some way contributed to a deeper understanding and connection to my sensual-sexuality. I encourage you to explore them to enrich and enhance your own process of sensual awakening.

Online Resources ~

Authentic Tantra.com- Authentic Tantra® Online Education is one of the most comprehensive online Tantric sex education programs in the world. Authentic Tantra.com is the ONLY school for Tantra offering The Secret Tibetan 5 Element Sexual Teachings.

Sex Toys For Tantra- sextoys4tantra.com was created as a resource for the readers of Shake Your Soul Song to provide the recommended "tools" for sensual transformation.

For Reading ~

The Sacred Female by Art Noble, Trafford Publishing, July 5, 2007

Women's Anatomy of Arousal by Sheri Winston, Mango Garden Press September 1, 2009

Female Ejaculation and the G-Spot: Not Your Mother's Orgasm Book! (Positively Sexual) by Deborah Sundahl, Hunter House, March 24, 2003

The Vagina: A New Biography by Naomi Wolf, Ecco

September 11, 2012

Emergence of The Sensual Woman~ Awakening Our Erotic Innocence by Saida Desilets, Jade Goddess Publishing , 2006

Non-Violent Communication~ A Language of Life by Marshal Rosenberg, Puddledancer Press, September 1, 2003

The Secrets Of The Ocean Breath by Carla Tara, June 23, 2011

Dance as a Healing Art by Anna Halprin, Life Rhythm, March 14, 2000

Emotional Anatomy by Stanley Keleman, Center Press Westlake Village, CA, June 1, 1989

For more resources please visit <u>www.authentictantra.com</u>

"The purpose of life, after all, is to live it,

to taste experience to the utmost,

to reach out eagerly and without fear

for newer and richer experience."

~ Eleanor Roosevelt ~

About the Author

Devi Ward Erickson is the Founder of the Institute of Authentic Tantra® Education, the first and only government accredited professional training institute using the Tibetan Five Element Tantric practices for holistic sexual healing. Devi is an ACS Certified Sexologist, Certified Tantric Healer, Certified Reiki Practitioner, Certified Meditation Instructor, and has been teaching meditation and personal growth workshops for over 20 years.

She is an author, and the Host of Sex is Medicine with Devi Ward Podcast on iTunes and tunein.com. She has been featured as a Tantric Healing Expert in countless articles and over 30 different radio and television networks world-wide including Playboy Radio, Men's Health Magazine, CBS, NBC and Rogers TV and the movie Sexology with Gabrielle Anwar and Catherine Oxenberg.

Devi's life mission is to spread the feminine wisdom that "Pleasure Is Medicine and Love has the Power to Heal".

Learn more at DeviWardTantra.com or AuthenticTantra.com.

Made in the USA
Middletown, DE
31 October 2022

13805596R00135